P9-BZD-174

The Day the World Exploded

SIMON WINCHESTER

The Day the World Exploded

The Earthshaking Catastrophe at Krakatoa

Adaptation by DWIGHT JON ZIMMERMAN

Collins
An Imprint of HarperCollinsPublishers

Rakata, the part of Krakatoa that survived the eruption of August 27, 1883, as seen from the summit of the cone of Anak Krakatau

Dwight Jon Zimmerman researched books, the Internet, and old print shops to find documents, etchings, paintings, and early photographs to illustrate the text, and he worked with the U.S. Geological Survey and individual photographers to add full-color photographs of volcanoes and volcanic activity.

"The Scream" © 2007 The Munch Museum/The Munch-Ellingsen Group/Artists Rights Society (ARS), NY: 73
Jeanie Barnett, www.cratertocirque.com: 4, 5, 16 (top), 78, 86, 88, 90, 91
R. Batalon, USAF, U.S. Geological Survey: 19 (top right)
Mike Byerly, Alaska Department of Fish and Game, Alaska Volcano Observatory: 13 (top)
Lynette Cook/Photoresearchers, Inc.: 67
The Cosmopolitan: 54 (lower right)
Cotteau: 70 (top)
Flammarion: 79
Game McGimsey, Alaska Volcano Observatory, U.S. Geological Survey: 57
R. Hadian, U.S. Geological Survey: 10
J. B. Judd, U.S. Geological Survey: 49 (bottom)
Library of Congress: 11, 18 (upper left), 29 (bottom), 35, 36 (both), 37 (both), 38 (both), 43 (left), 51 (bottom), 54 (top left)
NASA: 16 (bottom), 19 (bottom right), 22, 76, 92
National Archives: 65
National Oceanic & Atmospheric Administration: 7 (bottom right), 9, 23 (bottom), 61 (left)
D. L. Peck, Hawaii Volcanoes National Park, U.S. Geological Survey: 18 (upper right)
D. W. Peterson, U.S. Geological Survey: 49 (top)
Austin Post, U.S. Geological Survey: 19 (left)
Cyrus Read, Alaska Volcano Observatory, U.S. Geological Survey: 6 (top), 46, 64
Royal Delft, Holland: 45
Science and Society Picture Library: 81
Everett Skinner, Alaska Volcano Observatory, U.S. Geological Survey: 61
Soun Vannithone: 8, 15, 20, 41, 71
C. Stoughton, Hawaii Volcanoes National Park, U.S. Geological Survey: 17
Tropenmuseum, Amsterdam: 7 (upper right), 26 (upper left), 27 (top and bottom), 28 (both), 30 (top), 32, 33 (all), 48, 51 (upper right), 52, 59, 60, 68, 69 (top), 70 (bottom), 82, 85 (both), 86 (top), 87 (both)
U.S. Geological Survey: 18 (bottom)
R. D. M. Verbeek: 56 (top), 95
Wikipedia: 6 (bottom), 26 (bottom), 29 (top), 53
R. E. Wilcox, U.S. Geological Survey: 62
Harry Yeh, University of Washington, National Oceanic & Atmospheric Administration: 69 (bottom)
Dwight Jon Zimmerman: 13 (bottom), 23 (both), 25, 30 (bottom), 40 (top), 43 (right)

Collins is an imprint of HarperCollins Publishers.

Krakatoa: The Day the World Exploded: August 27, 1883
copyright © 2003 by Simon Winchester
Adaptation copyright © 2008 by Dwight Jon Zimmerman
Full-color illustrations on pages 2, 7, 12, 14, 15, 21, 24, 27, 31, 34, 39, 40, 42, 44, 47, 50, 55, 56, 58, 62, 65, 66, 73, 76, 80, 83, 84, 89 copyright © 2008 by Jason Chin

All rights reserved. Manufactured in China. No part of this book may be used or reproduced in any manner whatsoever without written permission except in the case of brief quotations embodied in critical articles and reviews. For information address HarperCollins Children's Books, a division of HarperCollins Publishers, 1350 Avenue of the Americas, New York, NY 10019.
www.harpercollinschildrens.com

Library of Congress Cataloging-in-Publication Data is available.
ISBN 978-0-06-123982-3 (trade bdg.) — ISBN 978-0-06-123983-0 (lib. bdg.)

Designed by Stephanie Bart-Horvath
1 2 3 4 5 6 7 8 9 10
❖
First Edition

For my first granddaughter, Coco

—S.W.

To my nieces, Julie and Gabrielle

—D.J.Z.

C O N T

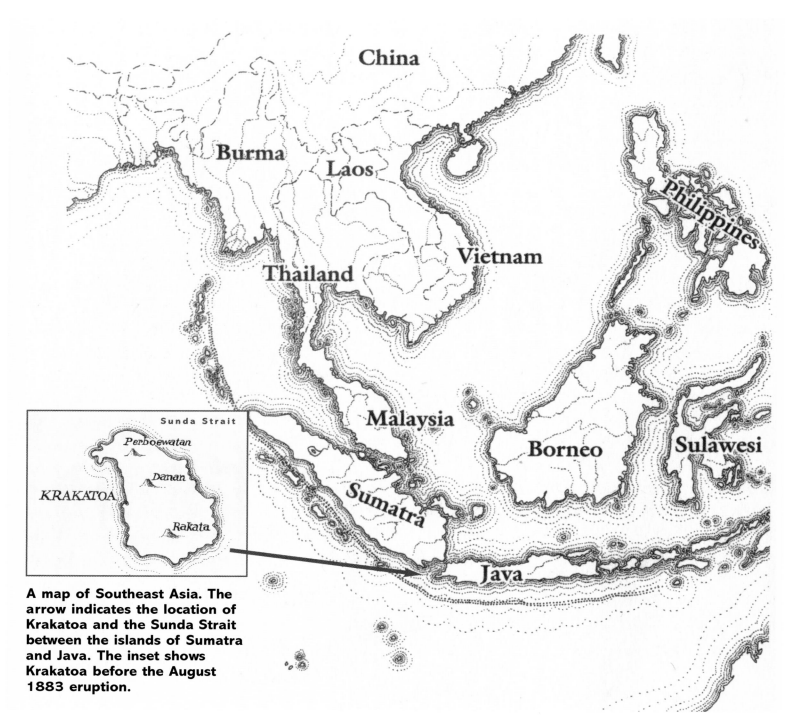

A map of Southeast Asia. The arrow indicates the location of Krakatoa and the Sunda Strait between the islands of Sumatra and Java. The inset shows Krakatoa before the August 1883 eruption.

The eruption of Krakatoa a century and a quarter ago remains an event burned indelibly into the public mind as one of the most terrifying examples of just what this planet can do when it sets its mind to it. It was a staggering, mind-blowing occurrence on all kinds of levels: it generated the loudest sound ever made, it sent pressure waves rushing around the world no fewer than seven times, it created tsunamis that killed more than thirty thousand people, and it stained the skies with lurid and frighteningly apocalyptic-looking colors for months afterward.

All of this had long fascinated me—from the time when, as a child, I read that wonderful American short story *Twenty-one Balloons*, in which Krakatoa figures, and then again when I saw the wonderfully awful Hollywood film *Krakatoa, East of Java*—awful in part because the geography of the title was so deliciously wrong: the island that was Krakatoa was actually *west* of Java.

So to do research for this book, I went by unauthorized fishing boat to the place—the belly of the beast—where it all happened. Three quite unrelated things about Krakatoa that I discovered in my researches left the greatest impression on me.

The first relates to how the event itself occurred at a most propitious time in the world's technological history. Eighteen years before, when Abraham Lincoln was assassinated in 1865, it took fully twelve days for the news to be sent from Washington, D.C., where the crime occurred, to newspaper readers in London. The telegraph took the signal only as far as Boston: the news then had to travel the rest of the way by boat. But by the time of Krakatoa's eruption on August 27, 1883, everything had changed. The world was now hooked together telegraphically by underwater cables. And this "Victorian internet" meant that the first telegraph signal—"Krakatoa erupts—many dead"—was received in London just a few *hours* after the volcano had exploded. Immediately the world started to become much, much more aware of itself—*the global village*, as it is now known, was born.

A lava flow

A nineteenth-century illustration of scientists measuring barometric pressure on the summit of the Puy de Dome in south-central France

Secondly, I found quite fascinating the process whereby life begins itself anew somewhere that has been totally and utterly ruined and made entirely lifeless. The tiny spider found after the island of Anak Krakatau rose from the ruins struck me as a symbol of hope. She had built her web for one reason only: she knew that, sooner or later, *a fly would come along.* She was a promise that, no matter how ruined, Nature would always, somehow, manage to revive itself.

Finally, the event marked the beginnings of a turning point in how humankind came to regard major natural catastrophes. In ancient times there was no doubt: an eruption, a mighty storm, a famine, a flood, an earthquake—all were clearly the works of an angry god. As late as 1755, when the city of Lisbon in Portugal was leveled by an immense quake, all believed it to be the work of God, and as a result hundreds of heretics—

Lightning strikes the stratovolcano Galunggung in Indonesia during an eruption.

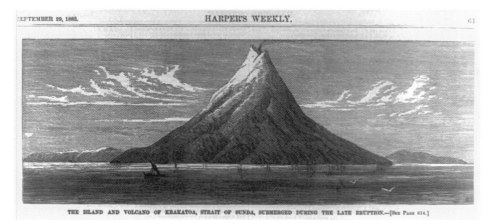

THE ISLAND AND VOLCANO OF KRAKATOA, STRAIT OF SUNDA, SUBMERGED DURING THE LATE ERUPTION.—[See Page 614.]

A *Harper's Weekly* illustration of Krakatoa before the August 1883 explosion

as non-Catholics were called—were burned at the stake as an apology. Much the same happened after Krakatoa. Local firebrand Islamic leaders said the eruption was Allah's doing, largely because the Javanese people had for so long submitted themselves to European rule (the country was a colony of the Netherlands). To placate Allah, westerners had thus to be killed—and many were in the first confrontation between militant Muslims and Christians in modern times. The rebellion, begun in the name of Krakatoa, was the first in a series that led to the expulsion of the Dutch in the 1950s and the creation of the Republic of Indonesia, which is today the most populous Islamic nation on the planet.

So the importance of Krakatoa goes well beyond the stunning nature of the event itself, for it affected the way we communicate, it enlarged our understanding of Nature, and it had immense implications both religious and political. Great natural disasters all too often lead to a cascade of unanticipated consequences. Hurricane Katrina is one more modern example. But Krakatoa was in this regard the mother of them all, with the world in all its savage beauty also reminding us of two important lessons. First, whatever we may do or whatever we may wish, Nature always gets its way. And second, *we humans inhabit this planet subject to geological consent, which can be withdrawn, without warning, at any time.*

—Simon Winchester

UNDERSTANDING VOLCANOES

Legends

Stripped of all drama, a volcano is nothing more than a pinhole in the earth's crust. But because that "pinhole" has such an awesome capacity for destruction, volcanoes became the source of terrifying myths and legends stretching back to mankind's earliest civilizations.

Some people living near volcanoes believed temperamental gods lived inside the fiery mountains. A volcano's eruption was a sign of anger. To please the god, people would throw a sacrifice into the volcano's crater. Usually that sacrifice was a young person or an animal, though sometimes flowers and fruit and harvested crops were used.

Eruption of the Alaskan volcano Augustine on May 26, 2006

THE SACRIFICE TO THE GODDESS PELE.

A nineteenth-century illustration showing Hawaiian natives making a sacrifice to the volcano goddess, Pele, whose lava is destroying their village

NEWS BRIEFS

▲ According to Polynesian legend, the Hawaiian Islands were created by the temperamental volcano goddess, Pele, who created the islands as a series of refuges to hide from her older sister Namakaokahai, the sea goddess, who constantly attacked her.

▲ In ancient Greek and Roman mythology, Mount Etna was the entrance to the underworld. It was also one of the forges used by the god Hephaestus (in Roman mythology the god Vulcan) to shape weapons, chariots, and other items for his fellow gods.

People once imagined that volcanic eruptions were caused by temperamental gods.

NEWS BRIEFS

▲ When Krakatoa began its activity, the natives in the area believed that Orang Alijeh, the much feared Javan god and mountain ghost, was angry and was going to soon punish people living in the region for offending him.

Eventually myth and legend gave way to science. The ancient Greek philosophers Anaxagoras and Aristotle expressed the idea that the source of a volcano's fury was wind trapped underground. Friction caused by the wind generated heat that melted the rock and created lava and magma. In ancient Rome, the philosopher Lucius Seneca said that the heat came from burning sulfur. It was a logical thought since people near an eruption commonly smelled sulfur.

During the seventeenth and eighteenth centuries, scientists used the then new and developing science of chemistry to try and explain how volcanoes worked. In the early 1800s, the common belief was that volcanic eruptions were caused by the oxidation of alkaline metals, particularly potassium, which in its pure form burns when exposed to air. But while this and other theories seemed to explain some of what happened, no single theory answered all the questions concerning volcanoes and their eruptions. The most tantalizing question remained: Why do rocks melt?

Alfred Wegener

Alfred Wegener was a famous German Arctic explorer and meteorologist. He was known as a generalist—someone interested in everything. And he was not afraid to step outside his chosen field to ask and answer questions he had about other sciences. In fact, he enjoyed it. In 1915 he created a firestorm of controversy when he published the theory he called "continental displacement," what we know today as "continental drift." Wegener was the first scientist to say that the earth's crust moved. This theory would later be important in explaining earthquakes and how volcanoes like Krakatoa were formed.

Though we now know that Wegener was right, his theory was rejected by all the scientific societies of the time. Sir Harold Jeffreys, an important geophysicist, claimed that no force could be powerful enough to move the earth's crust.

The first scientist to prove that Wegener's theory was correct was the American geologist Harry Hess. He had observed mysterious movements of rocks and sections of the sea floor along the ridges of undersea trenches. In 1939 Hess attempted to explain the cause. World War II interrupted his studies, and he was unable to return to the subject until 1962. This time, armed with additional research from other scientists, Hess wrote a paper for the Geological Society of America. His "History of Ocean Basins" has become a classic in the field. In it Hess states that continental drift is indeed taking place, with the continents moving like gigantic rafts, colliding and bouncing and plunging down back into the mantle, the earth's molten core. In 1965 University of Toronto professor J. Tuzo Wilson examined the characteristics of tectonic plates and conclusively proved Wegener's theory was correct.

Alfred Wegener died, apparently of a heart attack, shortly before his fiftieth birthday, on November 1, 1930, while on an expedition in Greenland. At the time his peers still believed that his ideas about continental drift were the results of bad science or wishful thinking. Yet his pioneering theory had answered one of the great geologic mysteries of history.

NEWS BRIEFS

▲ When he learned of Wegener's theory, the president of the American Philosophical Society called his theory "utter, damned rot!" And a respected British geologist said, "Anyone who valued his reputation for scientific sanity would never dare support such a theory."

▲ Wegener is memorialized by the names of two rare ice-crystal halo arcs and the Wegener-Bergeron-Findeisen procedure, the mechanism that creates the peculiar shape of raindrops, which Wegener helped to discover.

▲ J. Tuzo Wilson, a Canadian geophysicist and geologist, would later receive numerous honors and awards and be credited as the "father" of the new science of plate tectonics.

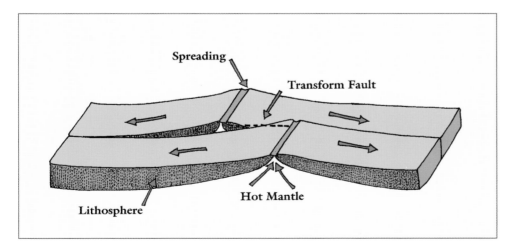

This is a diagram showing Professor J. Tuzo Wilson's plate tectonics principle of transform fault structure.

Alfred Wegener

Anak Krakatau, an example of a stratovolcano volcano

Mount Kilimanjaro, an example of a rift volcano

Science

Scientists now agree that there are at least twelve, and possibly as many as thirty-six, tectonic plates. These plates are constantly moving and bumping into each other. What happens exactly at the boundaries of these plates depends on a number of factors, including the composition and density of the rock and which way the plates are moving.

Tectonic plates are composed of two types of material, oceanic and continental. Oceanic material, essentially basalt, is heavy. Continental material is made of lighter rocks such as granite and sedimentary rock. When the two plates' density is not equal, a situation called subduction occurs. This means the denser oceanic plate slides below, or subducts, the lighter continental plate. As the oceanic plate is pushed down toward the hot molten core of the earth, it gradually melts and is absorbed by the mantle. In situations where the two rock plates have equal weight and density, the point where they meet is called a collision boundary. If they push together, the two plates create mountain ranges, like the Andes in South America, the Rocky Mountains in North America, the Alps in Europe, and the Himalayan Mountains in Asia. If the plates are moving away from each other, gigantic rifts are formed. This feature is most noticeable in maps that show the Great Rift Valley in eastern Africa and the Mid-Atlantic and East Pacific ocean floors.

The most common type of volcano is the stratovolcano—the classic cone-shaped volcano. The list includes Krakatoa and all the volcanoes in Indonesia, as well as Mount Fuji, Mount Pinatubo, Mount St. Helens, Mount Vesuvius, and Mount Etna, among others. Stratovolcanoes are formed in subduction zones—the place where two tectonic plates meet and where the heavier oceanic plate slides beneath the lighter continental plate. Fractures in the plates allow magma to surface and create stratovolcanoes.

A second type is the rift volcano. It is caused when two tectonic plates slide away from each other, creating an opening in the crust that allows magma to flow to the surface, much the same way blood flows out of a cut in the skin. The Great Rift Valley in eastern Africa is home to the famous volcano Mount Kilimanjaro, as well as Mount Kenya, Mount Nyiragongo, and others. The island nation of Iceland was formed by rift volcanic activity.

A third type of volcano is the hot spot volcano. The most famous of these are Mount Kilauea and Mauna Loa in Hawaii. They occur within a tectonic plate instead of at its edges and are, roughly, like holes punched into the middle of a piecrust—as the pie cooks, the steam and filling inside bubbles up through the opening.

NEWS BRIEFS

▲ Ninety percent of volcanoes that are expected to erupt are located in just nine countries—Indonesia, Japan, the United States, Russia, Chile, the Philippines, New Guinea, New Zealand, and Nicaragua.

Kilauea, an example of a hot spot volcano

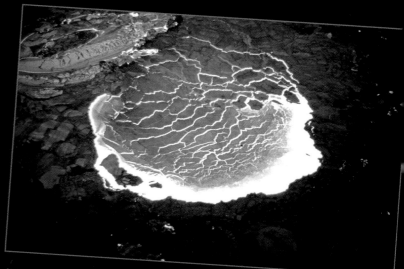

Mount Vesuvius, located near Naples, is the most famous active volcano in Europe because of its eruption in 79 a.d. that buried the Roman cities of Pompeii and Herculaneum. The most famous Roman to die in the eruption of Mount Vesuvius was Pliny the Elder, a naturalist who is famous for writing the thirty-seven-volume *Natural History*. As a memorial, his name is now a part of the vocabulary of volcanology. A Plinian eruption is a sudden, explosive eruption that destroys the volcano.

Kilauea, on the Island of Hawaii, is the youngest volcano in the Hawaiian Islands chain and has been erupting continuously since 1983. Escaping gases from Kilauea's eruptions create a condition know as "vog"—volcanic smog. Clouds of vog are formed when pollutants from the volcano, including sulfur dioxide, combine with oxygen and humidity in bright sunlight.

Mount Fuji, located on the Japanese island of Honshu, is perhaps the most beautiful volcano in the world. It is more than 100,000 years old, and its last recorded eruption occurred in 1708. It has been the subject of Japanese art and literature for centuries and is a popular tourist attraction, with more than 200,000 visitors each year. Mount Fuji has been used in the background of Godzilla movies and is a playable level in the popular *Shadow Hearts: Covenant* role-playing video game.

VOLCANOES

Mount Pinatubo, located on the island of Luzon in the Philippines, was a dormant volcano for 635 years before it erupted in June 1991 in the largest and most violent volcanic explosion of the twentieth century. More than two cubic miles of ash and gases were hurled into the atmosphere, causing global temperature to drop an average of about one degree Fahrenheit. More than 42,000 homes and 200,000 acres of land were destroyed. Thanks to early monitoring and large-scale evacuation efforts, only about 1,000 people died.

Mount St. Helens, located in western Washington State, is the most famous volcano in the continental United States. Its eruption in May 1980 reduced the height of the mountain by about 1,000 feet (from 9,677 feet to 8,365 feet), killed fifty-seven people, and destroyed 250 homes and forty-seven bridges. Ash from the eruption spread as far east as Minnesota and as far south as Oklahoma. One of the victims of the eruption was volcanologist David A. Johnson. He was in a mobile observation post about six miles north of Mount St. Helens when the volcano erupted. His radio message, "Vancouver! Vancouver! This is it!" was the first report of the eruption. It was also his last transmission, for he was killed minutes later by the volcano's blast.

Mount Etna, in Sicily, is the highest active volcano in Europe (about 10,900 feet) as well as one of the world's most active. Its earliest recorded eruption was in 1500 b.c., and more than 200 eruptions have taken place since then. Film footage of Mount Etna's eruptions in 2002–2003 was used as part of the landscape of the planet Mustafar in *Star Wars Episode III: Revenge of the Sith*.

NEWS BRIEFS

▲ The local word for the island is *Krakatau*, which is the name used by the scientific community for the original island and for Anak Krakatau, the small island that later emerged. The word *Krakatoa* is actually a mistake caused when the island's name was misspelled in telegraph dispatches about the eruption.

▲ *The Book of Ancient Kings* is possibly the longest book in the world. It took Ranggawarsita thirty years to write it, and the history contains six million words.

Ancient Krakatoa

The islands of Panjang, Sertung, Rakata, Danan, Perboewatan, and Polish Hat are believed to be remnants of Ancient Krakatoa, which exploded approximately sixty thousand years ago. Polish Hat became a small independent island, but volcanic buildup on Rakata, Danan, and Perboewatan eventually connected them, creating the Krakatoa volcano that exploded in 1883.

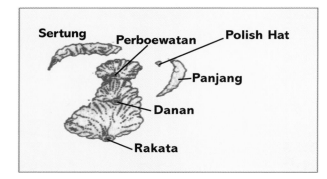

About Krakatoa

There is evidence that perhaps sixty thousand years ago or more there was a six-thousand-foot-high mountain that some geologists like to call Ancient Krakatau—or, as most people know it, Krakatoa. They believe it was centered on an almost perfectly circular island about nine miles in diameter. But then a gigantic eruption, witnessed only by Aboriginal ancestors, if indeed by anyone, may have devastated the island and its peak.

Once the dust had settled, what remained of Ancient Krakatoa was a group of small islands. At the northern end of the group were two low crescent-shaped skerries, or rocky islands—Panjang, about three miles long, and Sertung, about four miles long, and a tiny island called Polish Hat. Rakata, Danan, and Perboewatan eventually joined into a larger piece, six miles long, called Krakatoa. There were three volcano cones on Krakatoa: 2,667-foot Rakata in the south; 1,460-foot Danan, roughly in the middle; and at only 400 feet, Perboewatan, the lowest, on the northern tip.

How active were the volcano cones? Record-keeping among the early civilizations in the area mixed myth, legend, and fact in such an intricate way that it is hard to separate the truth from the fanciful tale. Most modern history books agree that humans possibly saw eruptions at Krakatoa in 416 a.d., 535 a.d., and 1680 a.d.

The most frequently quoted source for the first, and possibly the second, eruption is *The Book of Ancient Kings*, written in the nineteenth century by Raden Ngabahi Ranggawarsita, a poet in the Javanese royal court. Many scientists who studied the passages are convinced that he made up the 416 a.d. event, particularly since he rewrote these passages two years after Krakatoa's 1883 eruption.

But many believe that some kind of titanic event occurred at or near Krakatoa around 535 a.d. Dating of ice cores and tree rings is highly accurate, and these records show that, sometime between the years 510 and

560 a.d., a major event occurred, like a volcanic eruption, that scattered dust in the air around the world and reduced its temperature.

The eruption in 1680 a.d. was reported by three Europeans: John Vilhelm Vogel, a silver assayer; Elias Hesse, a writer; and a captain of a trading ship whose name is lost to history. Unfortunately their accounts contain numerous exaggerations, and there is a lack of confirming records from official sources.

Despite an overall lack of definite proof, legends of Krakatoa's eruptions in the distant past were a part of the lore of the region, regarded as colorful local stories by the Europeans.

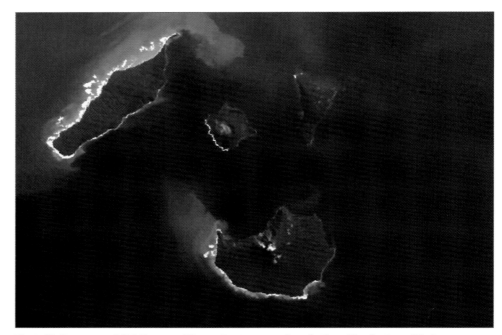

Detail from a 1992 satellite photograph of the Krakatau Volcano National Park, part of Indonesia's Ujung Kulon National Park, showing the islands of Sertung (left), Anak Krakatau (middle), Panjang (right), and Rakata (bottom)

Jan van Schley's etching shows two ships passing what is presumed to be Krakatoa during the eruption of 1680.

Homme de java

An etching of a Javanese man

A BUSINESS EMPIRE

The Spice Trade

For centuries merchants risked their fortunes, pirates risked their lives, and kings and sultans fought for control over the holy trinity of the Asian spice trade—pepper, clove, and nutmeg. Along with other exotic spices like mace, these were grown only in the Indies (at first India, but then later Malaysia, Java, Sumatra, and other islands in the archipelago).

This made Sunda Strait one of the busiest sea lanes in the world. And Krakatoa is located in the middle of it.

The importance of these spices is no exaggeration. Two hundred years before the birth of Christ, the Chinese people of the Han Dynasty demanded that their courtiers address their emperors only when their breath had been sweetened with a mouthful of Javanese cloves. Ancient Romans used nutmeg as incense. And in Elizabethan England of the sixteenth century, nutmeg was believed to be effective in keeping away the plague.

European demand for pepper, clove, and nutmeg not only survived the fall of the Roman Empire, the rise and fall of the Byzantine Empire, the Crusades, and assorted political and religious conflicts of the Middle Ages, it grew. It was the economic desire to find a shorter, and thus cheaper, route to the Indies that led Italian sea captain Christopher Columbus, who was working for Spain, to sail west. Unfortunately for him, the earth was considerably larger than he imagined and the American continents lay between him and his goal. Meanwhile his seafaring rivals working for Portugal, among them Vasco da Gama and Pedro Cabral, sailed south around the tip of Africa and then east to India and the Indies.

For most of the 1500s, the spice trade was dominated by the Portuguese, who set up colonies, like outposts, on the coasts of Africa and Asia. Portuguese merchants grew rich and jealously guarded their trade through a combination of exclusive treaties and military forts. But with so much money to be made by importing spice, it was inevitable that competitors would find a way to break the Portuguese monopoly in the spice trade.

An early etching of a Javanese couple in front of their home

The Sultan of Jogjakarta

The Dutch East Indies Company

In 1602 the Dutch government made history in the business world when it formally chartered a trading cooperative named Vereenigde Oost-Indische Compagnie, later known by the initials VOC and, in English, as the Dutch East Indies Company. The Dutch East Indies Company would be recognized as the world's first international corporation.

The government gave the company the exclusive right to conduct business east of the Cape of Good Hope in South Africa. More importantly it also gave the company the power to act like an independent government in the territories where it did business. This meant it could sign its own treaties with sultans and other local rulers, build forts, create and maintain armed forces, and set up administrative systems of governments. In return officials had to pledge loyalty to the Dutch government.

The European headquarters of the Dutch East Indies Company in Amsterdam

The Sultan of Jogjakarta and his entourage, together with Dutch colonial officials during an Islamic religious festival

A royal Javanese bride's wedding procession

▲ The most important spice from the Indies was pepper. Each year the Romans sent a merchant fleet of about 120 ships to the Indies to purchase pepper. The Romans bought so much of the spice that Pliny the Elder complained that Rome was going to go broke buying pepper because each year the empire spent more than fifty million sesterces on it.

▲ Any comparison between the values of ancient currencies to those of today is at best a guess. One way to estimate uses the total money value of all goods produced by country, the Gross Domestic Product (GDP). For instance, in Pliny the Elder's time, fifty million sesterces was about one percent of Rome's GDP. In comparison, one percent of the GDP of the United States in 2000 was 98.17 billion dollars.

▲ When the barbarian Alaric the Visigoth and his hordes laid siege to Rome in the fifth century, he demanded from the city a ransom of more than a ton of pepper.

▲ Ancient Egyptians used pepper in their mummies. The nostrils of the pharaoh Ramses II were found to contain black peppercorns.

NEWS BRIEFS

▲ Heading the Dutch East Indies Company was a board of directors composed of seventeen men, known as the Gentlemen Seventeen, who had absolute rule. They were so successful that the VOC had near-exclusive control of all business in the East Indies for almost two centuries, from 1602 to 1799.

▲ The Dutch East Indies Company suffered from bad management and financial setbacks in the late eighteenth century and went bankrupt in 1800. The company was then taken over by the government, and its officials became government employees.

▲ The original headquarters for the first three VOC governor-generals in the Indies was on the island of Ambon. Even though the island was close to where the spices were grown, it was far from the main trade routes on the western side of the Indies. Thus, Governor-General Coen decided he had to move.

▲ In the Javanese language, *Jayakarta* means "victorious and prosperous." After Indonesia gained its independence from the Dutch in 1949, the Indonesians changed the name of Batavia to Jakarta, a modernized form of the city's original name, and made the city the new nation's capital.

A Dutch controleur, seated middle, poses with the Sultan of Borneo, seated to his left.

A VOC letter of credit

The company's boss in the Dutch East Indies was called a governor-general. The most famous was the fourth man to hold the position, Jan Pieterszoon Coen, one of the company's founders. Coen became governor-general in 1618 and quickly began expanding the VOC's power. He decided that the two established commercial cities in the area, Malacca and Banteen, were not suitable sites for the business empire he was planning. The problem with Malacca was that the rival Portuguese were using it as their headquarters, and Coen did not want competitors as his next-door neighbors. Banteen was rejected because the sultan was capricious and could be counted on only to make trouble. However, the sultan had allowed the Dutch to build a small port on the right bank of the sluggish Ciliwung River opposite a village called Jayakarta. Since this location was far enough away from the disruptive influence of the sultan and the prying eyes of the Portuguese, Coen decided to build his headquarters there.

The city that rose up around the new headquarters was called Batavia. It quickly became one of the great colonial capitals of the world.

Front and back images
of a VOC coin

A view of a Dutch harbor in Rotterdam in the late 1800s

▲ Batavia was the old name for the Netherlands, taken from the Roman name for the local tribes, the Batavians, or Batavi.

▲ Slaves were imported to make life more comfortable for the Dutch. The wealthier Dutchmen might have as many as one hundred of them. The slaves arrived from Malaya, India, Burma, and Bali and were put to work as household servants in such roles as lamplighters, coachmen, page boys, tea makers, bakers, and seamstresses.

▲ A Town Hall was built in Batavia where official business was conducted aboveground. There were dungeons below. Later many stories were told of how the VOC security officers resorted to torturing their prisoners to obtain confessions.

A Javanese boat on a river in western Java

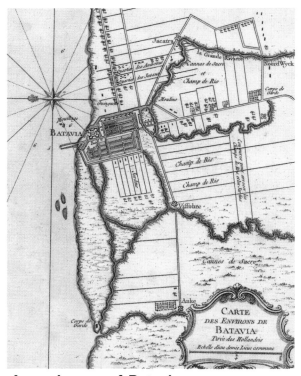

An early map of Batavia

Batavia

Batavia was located at the mouth of the Ciliwung River on the northwest shore of Java, about a hundred miles east of Krakatoa. The first Dutch settlers who arrived there in the early 1600s were by and large rather frightened men, understandably bewildered by the tropical heat, humidity, smells, and jungle so different from their native Netherlands. They re-created familiar scenes on this foreign shore, beginning with a fortress, a prison, an armory, a treasury, a Protestant church, and a small palace for the company's governor-general.

But that was just the beginning of their construction effort. They dredged the lagoon and expanded the size of the settlement. The Ciliwung River was straightened and bordered by large embankments of dirt. Classic Dutch drawbridges were then constructed to connect residents on both sides of the river. They built a network of narrow streets and sixteen canals. The canals were lined with flowering tamarind trees to remind the settlers of home. Then local crocodiles got into the habit of swimming in the canals and walking along its banks and poking their noses into the doorways of the homes that lined the canals.

A painting of the exotic botanic garden at Buitenzorg. The governor-general's palace is in the background.

Under the sure, if strict, rule of Governor-General Coen and his successors, Batavia rapidly grew into a major center of international commerce. Warehouses along the harbor were filled and emptied and filled again with teak and mahogany, spices, silks, and goods of an incredible and colorful variety. And mansion after mansion was built, complete with wrought-iron gates, gilded carvings, and Delft tiles, for the men who became rich off the company's trade. As the city grew, the small European population moved out of the hot and humid company town up to the relatively more agreeable climate in the hills, where they built an exclusive neighborhood named Buitenzorg, "Without a Care." By the 1880s more than a million people lived in and around Batavia; only about 12,000 were European.

A painting of a scenic road near Buitenzorg

Having captured a large crocodile, Dutch hunters pose with a family on Java.

A Dutch home in the East Indies with the family and domestic staff posing before it

AMAZING CENTURY

Discovery and Invention

The nineteenth century was a time of breathtaking scientific, social, and technological revolution and revelation. It began with British scientist Henry Cavendish calculating, for the first time, the density of the earth, and Johann Bode of Germany publishing *Uranographia*, an atlas of stars and nebulae. It ended with the German scientist Max Planck issuing his landmark quantum theory and Danish scientist Niels Bohr publishing his theory of atomic structure. Even the word *technology* was coined for the first time—by Jacob Bigelow in his *The Elements of Technology*.

The century included such giants of science and technology as William Thomson (Lord Kelvin), Louis Pasteur, Christian Doppler, Thomas Edison, Alexander Graham Bell, James Joule, and many others whose names live on through their discoveries, their inventions, the scientific principles and theories they proposed, or the species of flora and fauna they discovered.

Truly, the variety was breathtaking. William Kelly and Henry Bessemer perfected the smelting processes that removed impurities in steel manufacture. Now steel alloys could be used to make everything from trains and the rails on which they traveled, to weapons of destruction, to delicate scientific instruments to measure and record and make visible that which is invisible to the human eye. Inventions such as Isaac Singer's sewing machine (invented in 1851) and Eberhard Faber's mass-produced pencil (1861) enriched day-to-day life. Exploring new frontiers in the heavens, French physicist Armand Fizeau calculated the speed of light. Matthew F. Maury's *The Physical Geography of the Sea* (published in 1855) established the science of oceanography.

Samuel Colt, Horace Smith and Daniel Wesson, Richard Gatling, Louis Maxim, Alfred Nobel, and the Krupp steel foundry family created new and more powerful weapons and explosives that mankind used against itself. Meanwhile, Louis Pasteur, Joseph Lister, Ignaz P. Semmelweis, Florence

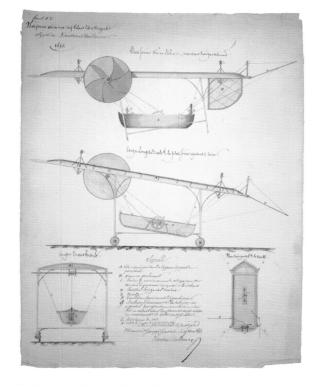

A design for a dirigible powered by manually operated propellers

▲ Thomas Edison filed more than 1,000 patents during his lifetime. Among his many inventions were the lightbulb and the motion picture camera. By the time he became an adult, Edison was completely deaf. Several reasons were given for its cause, including a bout of scarlet fever, a series of ear infections that were never treated, and the impact of blows delivered by an angry train conductor when Edison's chemical lab in a boxcar caught fire.

▲ Louis Pasteur's sterilization process, pasteurization, was originally created to help the French wine industry. Later it was used on milk.

▲ Dr. Joseph Lister, an English surgeon, was the first to use carbolic acid to sterilize surgical instruments and clean wounds. Thanks to this and other practices he advocated, postsurgical deaths were dramatically reduced. He was later made a baron, and the mouthwash Listerine is named after him.

▲ By the end of the century, more than a million miles of telephone lines had been strung in the United States.

A steam-powered tram in Batavia

A sewing machine advertisement showing a couple from Ceylon and two sewing machines

Nightingale, and others bettered and extended human lives with advances in surgery, health care, and the discovery of the sources of disease.

No longer was transportation limited to walking or riding a horse or animal-drawn wagon, or dependent on the whims of the wind and the power of a pulled oar. On land the steam locomotive went from a noisy curiosity to a necessity for the rapid transport of people and goods. On water Robert Fulton's paddle-wheeled steamboat gave way to the globe-spanning steamship. And in the air Henri Giffard, Dupuy de Lome, Charles F. Ritchel, and others were designing and flying fragile, balloon-shaped airships, a foretaste of airplanes to come in the twentieth century.

Recording scientific achievements soon extended beyond the confines of scientific societies. Popular journals such as *Scientific American*, founded in 1845, and *Popular Science*, founded in 1872, were among the many periodicals created to satisfy the common individual's passion for the latest news and developments in the world of science.

The paradox was that with this increase in knowledge came the humbling, and—for some—frightening realization that there was so much more about the world that remained a mystery. Advances in communications technology—the telegraph, undersea telegraph cables, and news agencies—gave people same-day knowledge of Krakatoa's eruption. But at the same time, limited geological knowledge made it impossible to answer people wondering if, when, and where the next great volcanic explosion would occur.

These nineteenth-century illustrations reflect the fascination held by many people for the new inventions being created. At top is a poster for a musical comedy *The Air Ship*, and at bottom is a Currier and Ives lithograph of a pair of steamboats.

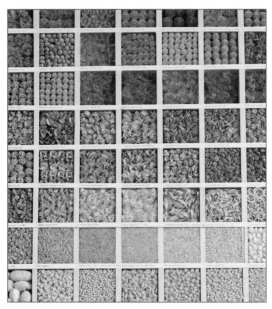

A seed specimen display

A butterfly specimen display

The Wallace Line

Charles Darwin is the British naturalist who is known as the founder of the science of evolution. But some scientists claim the real founder is a Welshman: Alfred Russel Wallace.

Wallace was born in the town of Usk in South Wales in 1823. The seventh child of a librarian, he began work as a schoolteacher in Leicestershire, England. Later he became a geographer. His main hobby was collecting and cataloging beetles and researching their activities. In 1848 Wallace and his friend Henry Walter Bates took their small savings and traveled to the Amazon rain forest of Brazil to study and gather beetles and insects there. That trip ended in disaster. On the return voyage, their ship caught fire and sank, and Wallace lost all his specimens and notes. But during his explorations, Wallace had formed two important beliefs: that geography influenced what types of plants and animals could exist in a region and that individual species developed through a process we now call evolution. He wrote two books on the subject that were read by Darwin. But because Wallace had only his memory as a resource, the books were thin on the hard facts scientists need. Still, this setback did not discourage him.

In 1854 Wallace boarded a ship for the East Indies. During his eight years there, Wallace meticulously organized a collection of close to 125,000 specimens of plants, animals, insects, and birds he found on the islands. There were 310 mammals, 100 reptiles, 8,000 birds, 13,000 butterflies, 7,500 seashells, 13,000 assorted insects, and, not surprisingly given his passion, 83,000 beetles. He had quite a few adventures. On the island of Lombok, he survived a frightening encounter with a group of headhunters. As a result of his treks through swamps and rain forests, his arms and legs became badly infected by leeches and biting insects. On the island of Ambon he discovered himself sharing his hut with a ten-foot

NEWS BRIEFS

▲ In recognition of Wallace's discovery, the line where the Asian and Australian continental shelves meet was named the Wallace Line. Also named after him are: a trench off Java, a 13,300-foot mountain in the Sierra Nevada, a garden in Wales, an aviary in Bristol, a bird of paradise, biology prizes in both Kansas and Australia, numerous lecture theaters and university halls, and craters on both Mars and the Moon.

▲ Because Darwin became more famous than Wallace for the theory of evolution, for many years Wallace was called Darwin's Moon.

▲ During his lifetime, Wallace did have advocates in respected scientific circles including the geologist Charles Lyell and the botanist Joseph Dalton Hooker. They persuaded Darwin to share some of the glory regarding the theory of evolution with Wallace.

▲ Wallace was never bitter over the fact that Darwin became more famous. In fact, Wallace coined the word Darwinism for the theory of evolution.

Alfred Russel Wallace

The deer-like Rusa is a native of the island of Timor.

snake curled up in its rafters. And he repeatedly suffered attacks of tropical diseases including dysentery and malaria.

Wallace took great care in writing down his observations, noting in detail every fact he knew about a specimen, including where it lived as well as where it did not. This strict difference of habitat would become an important clue to geologists in later years. One of his most profound discoveries was that there were two wholly different groups of plants and animals living in the Indies. There seemed to be a border, or dividing line, that separated the colony into two distinct regions. On the western side of the line were mammals: apes and monkeys, flying lemurs, tigers, wolves, civets, mongooses, deer, and the like. On the eastern side of the line were the marsupials: kangaroos, opossums, wombats, and duck-billed platypuses. This difference extended to birds and plants as well. The dividing line ran approximately northeast to southwest. It began at Mindanao, the large, southernmost island of the Philippines, and continued down to the island now known as Sulawesi, passing between Sulawesi in the east and Borneo in the west, and extending south between Lombok (east) and Bali (west)—islands that are only fifteen miles apart.

In one of his journals, Wallace wrote: "The contrast is nowhere so abruptly exhibited as on passing from the island of Bali to that of Lombok. . . . In Bali we have barbets, fruit-thrushes, and woodpeckers; on passing over to Lombok these are seen no more, but we have an abundance of cockatoos, honeysuckers, and brush-turkeys, which are equally unknown in Bali and every island further west."

What Wallace realized was that the reason these two biologically distinct regions had come so close but remained so different was because of geology. Wallace became more and more excited about his discovery and would spend many years writing articles trying to explain his theory. Though he had no way of proving it during his lifetime, Wallace had discovered the meeting place of two continental shelves. His efforts had provided the first clues to the study of plate tectonics in the twentieth century.

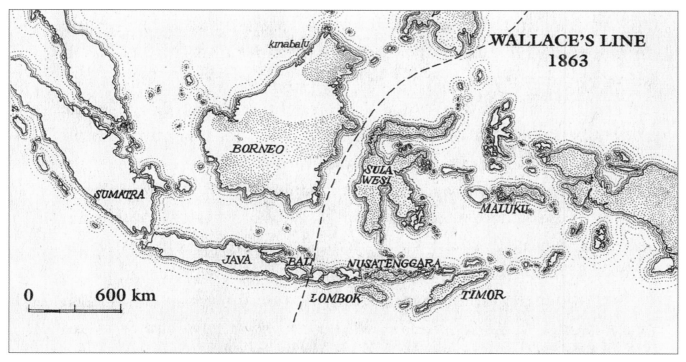

A map showing the location of the Wallace Line where two continental shelves meet

Samuel Morse and his telegraph

The Telegraph

Samuel Morse, the man whose invention would send news of the Krakatoa explosion to all corners of the earth, began his adult life as an aspiring portrait painter. He sailed from America to Europe to further his art education in Italy, Switzerland, and France. On the return voyage home in 1832, Morse met Dr. Charles Jackson, an expert in electromagnetism. During the six weeks of their ocean voyage, Dr. Jackson demonstrated to Morse a number of experiments in electromagnetism, including a form of electromagnetic communication. Morse was fascinated. Before their ship reached the American shore, he had formed rough plans for a telegraph.

Morse soon teamed up with Professor Leonard Gale and Alfred Vail and with their help began work on creating a practical electronic telegraph. In 1842 Congress funded an experimental telegraph line. In 1845 his Magnetic Telegraph Company was founded, and soon telegraph lines were being laid all across the United States.

The Magnetic Telegraph Company had a number of competitors, especially in Europe, each with its own signaling method. Morse's competition was effectively swept away when, in 1851, European nations adopted his equipment and Morse code system as the standard for telegraph communications. From that point on, the Morse code system became the standard for the world.

In 1856 the first telegraph lines connected the Dutch East Indies Company's palace in Buitenzorg to its offices in Batavia. By 1870 Batavia was connected by underwater telegraph cables to Australia and the Malay States and through them to a network that spanned the world. Before the arrival of the telegraph, news between Batavia and the Netherlands had to be carried by ships, with weeks passing between arrival and departure. Now news could travel across the globe within hours. The importance of that fact would be fully realized in 1883.

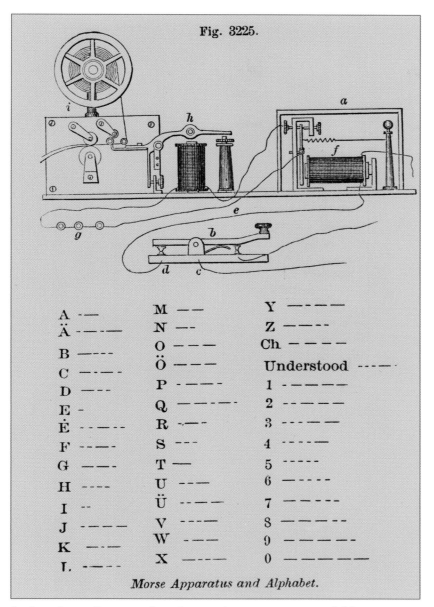

Fig. 3225.

A ·—	M ——	Y —·——
Ä ·—·—	N —·	Z ——··
B —···	O ———	Ch ————
C —·—·	Ö ———·	Understood ···—·
D —··	P ·——·	1 ·————
E ·	Q ——·—	2 ··———
É ··—··	R ·—·	3 ···——
F ··—·	S ···	4 ····—
G ——·	T —	5 ·····
H ····	U ··—	6 —····
I ··	Ü ··——	7 ——···
J ·———	V ···—	8 ———··
K —·—	W ·——	9 ————·
L ·—··	X —··—	0 —————

Morse Apparatus and Alphabet.

A drawing of an early telegraph apparatus and Morse code alphabet

NEWS BRIEFS

▲ The first known type of telegraph was the "optical telegraph." It used smoke signals, light beacons, and semaphore flags that flashed coded messages from one station to another.

▲ Morse's big break as a portrait artist came in 1825 when he was commissioned to paint a full-length portrait of the Marquis de Lafayette.

▲ Samuel Morse was not the first to invent the electrical telegraph. Spanish physician and scientist Francisco de Salva invented the first known telegraph in the late 1700s. A small telegraph service between two railway stations was used in Great Britain in 1839.

▲ Morse code is a signaling system that uses a series of short and long electronic pulses—"dots" and "dashes"—to form letters that are combined with precisely measured pauses that separate letters, words, and sentences.

Side and cross-section views of an undersea telegraph cable. The telegraph cables are in the center; the outer ring of cables is a series of support wires. The black material is a waterproof substance called gutta percha.

EARLY WARNINGS

May 1883

Before 1883, anyone living along the clean white beaches of Java and Sumatra that bordered the Sunda Strait believed Krakatoa was peaceful—an extinct, or at least inactive, volcano. It was a place far removed from the active volcanoes of Merapi, Merbapu, or Bromo in central and east Java.

But just after midnight on the morning of Thursday, May 10, 1883, the lighthouse keeper at what was then called First Point, about thirty miles south of Krakatoa on the far southwestern tip of Java, felt a tremor. A new chapter in Krakatoa's history was about to begin. The lighthouse suddenly seemed to shift on its foundations. The sea abruptly whitened, appeared to freeze briefly, and became uncannily smooth like a mirror. Then it shivered slightly and returned to its usual swell of waves. There was no hint of where the vibration began. The keeper checked his records: The last volcano to erupt anywhere nearby was Lamongan, six hundred miles east. He wrote about the incident in his log book and included it in the weekly summary that he sent to his superiors in Batavia.

Five days later, on the night of May 15, another set of vibrations occurred. This time they were stronger, more sustained, and felt not only in western Java but also across the Sunda Strait in eastern Sumatra. Controller Willem Beyerinck, an official in the Dutch government's colonial service stationed in the coastal town of Ketimbang, was awakened by the rumblings and shakings. He immediately wrote a telegram to his superiors at the government headquarters in Batavia. But he was reluctant to send it because he was afraid that his emotions had gotten the best of him, and that as a result he may have exaggerated. Five days later, on Sunday, May 20, he finally decided to send it. Marked confidential so that only his superiors, including the colony's top government official, Governor-General Frederick s' Jacob, would be told of its contents, it reported that powerful tremors were being felt continuously up and down the Sumatran coast on

NEWS BRIEFS

▲ Seismic events, including earthquakes and volcanic eruptions, were commonplace in the Indies. But the year 1883 opened rather quietly, seismically speaking. Between January and May, the observatory at Batavia had logged only fourteen earthquakes, and of these four were in eastern Java and seven in Sumatra, all far away from Krakatoa.

▲ Delft is a city in the southern part of the Netherlands. It is famous for its distinctive blue-and-white pottery called Delftware or Delft pottery.

▲ A controller, or *contrôleur* in Dutch, is a junior-grade civil servant in the Dutch colonial service responsible for the administration of a territory subdivision known as a department. Though an official with low rank, a controller possessed immense authority, and the screening process was rigorous. In order to qualify for service in the Dutch East Indies, a controller had to be a college graduate, pass a series of examinations to prove his proficiency in a number of languages, both European and native, and be knowledgeable in local and international law, algebra, geometry, trigonometry, geology, drawing, land surveying, and a number of other disciplines. They were, as might be expected, serious individuals whose advice and information carried great weight.

A steam cloud rises out of a volcano's crater.

the northern and western sides of the Sunda Strait. This was the first official word that something unusual was happening in the area.

On that same Sunday, Captain Hollman of the German ship *Elizabeth* was on the ship's bridge looking at the southern summit of Krakatoa as his ship slowly made its way through the Sunda Strait. At 10:30 a.m., he suddenly got the surprise of his life. He later wrote that, without warning: ". . . we saw from the island a white cumulus cloud, rising fast. It rose almost vertically until, after about half an hour, it had reached a height of about 11,000 meters. Here it started to spread like an umbrella . . . so that soon only a small part of the blue sky was seen on the horizon. When at about 4:00 in the afternoon a light south-southeast breeze started, it brought a fine ash dust which increased strongly . . . until the entire ship was covered in all parts with a uniform fine grey dust layer."

Captain Hollman was the first European to see Krakatoa's first eruption. Father Heims, his ship's chaplain, wrote that "the ship, which was so clean 24 hours ago . . . looked like a floating cement factory. . . . covered uniformly with a grey sticky dust."

An important third record of what happened that Sunday was made by Dr. J. P. van der Stok, who lived in the old part of Batavia. Dr. van der Stok was in his living room reading the newspaper at the time. Suddenly an expensive Delft porcelain dinner plate, part of Mrs. van der Stok's wedding trousseau, fell off the dinner table and shattered. All the windows and doors in the house began to shake and rattle. From somewhere to the west the doctor heard a low, rumbling sound, like that of distant artillery. He pulled out his pocket watch and noted the time: 10:55 a.m.

Dr. van der Stok was a distinguished scientist who was the director of the Dutch colony's Magnetic and Meteorological Observatory. He promptly walked over to the observatory, which was attached to the house, to check his scientific instruments. The needles and pens on the magnetic declinometer were ticking and trembling violently. But what was unusual was that instead of side-to-side sweeps that one might expect from an earthquake, the needles and pens were moving in a series of buzzing up-and-down motions, an action that could not be registered properly on the instrument. As Dr. van der Stok thought about it, he realized something truly odd was happening. The vibrations were not so much being felt though his feet, as if coming from deep in the earth, as they were being felt in the air. Also, unlike earthquake vibrations, which are brief, the vibrations had been going on for an hour and showed no signs of stopping.

Worried Batavians soon arrived at his door, anxiously wanting to know what was going on. Dr. van der Stok gave answers that seemed to calm them, at least outwardly.

But what did the vibrations really mean?

Vibrations from Krakatoa were so strong they caused Mrs. van der Stok's Delftware plate to fall off the table.

▲ Prior to the age of computers, the Internet, and blogging, the writing of diaries was very popular, especially in the nineteenth and early-to-mid-twentieth centuries. Up until the mid-twentieth century diary-keeping was mostly done by the upper and middle classes, who had both the necessary time and education to be able to do so.

▲ Few of the Dutch East Indies houses, even those of the wealthy, had indoor plumbing. As a result, water for cooking, washing, and other uses was stored in large barrels.

Merchant ships at anchor in a bay in an island in the Dutch East Indies

Perboewatan Erupts

On Sunday mornings, Mrs. Willem Beyerinck was in the habit of sitting on her veranda in Ketimbang, which had a magnificent view of Sunda Strait. She enjoyed watching the many ships that passed by. On May 20, she was jolted from her routine by a series of hammer blow–like tremors. She immediately began writing her observations in her diary. She noted that the vibrations were best seen in the water barrels kept stored in the bathroom, since their surfaces rippled prettily with every detonation.

As she continued her writing, a native fishing boat arrived unannounced, and the frightened fishermen rushed up to the house to see the controller, Mr. Beyerinck. In a mixture of Sundanese, the local language, and pidgin Dutch, they explained that they had gone to Krakatoa to gather wood for boat building. While they were felling trees, they suddenly heard what sounded like cannon fire from a warship practicing its gunnery in the strait. When a second explosion occurred, this time terrifyingly loud and close, they ran down to the beach and saw the very beach itself split wide open. Jets of black ash and red-hot stones roared out into the air.

Mrs. Beyerinck was in no mood to listen to excitable natives. She told her husband, acidly, that it was simply impossible for a beach to erupt. But then Mr. Beyerinck's superior, Mr. Altheer, arrived from his colonial government headquarters in Telok Betong, further up the bay. He told Beyerinck that the governor-general in Batavia had sent a telegram ordering him to find out what was going on with Krakatoa, as he was receiving many alarming reports.

Beyerinck and Altheer promptly boarded their official government boat and headed south for Krakatoa. The sea was rough and choppy, and they passed wave after wave of floating pumice stone and numerous charred and floating trees. They were drenched by sudden high waves, enveloped in clouds of choking gas, and repeatedly covered by falling ash. It took them four hours—not the expected two—to reach Krakatoa.

Lava erupting

Their records do not indicate for certain whether or not they actually landed on the island. But they saw exactly what had so frightened the fishermen. The northernmost beach of Krakatoa was belching fire and smoke. The smallest and most northerly of Krakatoa's three volcanic cones, Perboewatan, was erupting—getting stronger with every minute. The Dutch colonial officials turned their boat around and headed back to Ketimbang, where they sent a report by telegraph marked for the eyes of the governor-general only.

Two days later, the ominous rumbling on Krakatoa stopped. Only a thin plume of white smoke and steam continued to rise above the Perboewatan crater, a hint that something continued to roil deep within the earth.

Tourism

The ongoing volcanic activity on Krakatoa fascinated the local European population, and ship owners saw an opportunity to profit. The Netherlands Indies Steamship Company was the first to come up with an excursion. On Saturday, May 26, 1883, representatives from the company tacked up notices in two of the most popular gathering places of Batavian society, the Harmonie and Concordia Clubs, advertising the delights of an "agreeable excursion" aboard the *Gouverneur-Generaal Loudon* for only twenty-five guilders per ticket (which, at approximately ten dollars, made it affordable only to the more wealthy). By Sunday morning the *Loudon* was fully booked, with 86 passengers. The party set off that evening, seventeen days after the first vibration, only a week after the first eruption.

After steaming through the night toward the "purple, fiery glow" that was Krakatoa, the passengers were on deck when dawn broke. As the government's representative, Mr. A. L. Schuurman, a mining engineer, later reported: "The view of the island was fantastic: it was bare and dry, instead of rich with tropical forests, and smoke rose from it like smoke coming from ovens. Only the high peak [of Rakata] had some green left, but the flat

The Concordia Military Club

NEWS BRIEFS

▲ The Harmonie and Concordia Clubs were the competing centers of Batavian high society in the Dutch East Indies. The Concordia Club, more formally known as the Concordia Military Club, was younger than the Harmonie Club. It was located in a grand white marble building directly across from the governor-general's palace. It was famous for its elaborate masked balls. For one, a large, fancy fountain was set up in the center of the ballroom. But instead of water, the fountain gushed pure eau de cologne.

Typical transportation for natives in the Dutch East Indies was a two-wheeled cart drawn by buffalo.

One of the last known photographs of Krakatoa before its eruption

NEWS BRIEFS

▲ For all its wealth, Batavian high society still suffered (if that can be said) from not being able to have the same things that they did back in the Netherlands. One of those items was beef. Because refrigeration equipment did not exist, meat from cattle was an impossible-to-obtain luxury. On July 20, 1883, the British steamship *Fiado* arrived at Batavia. Its refrigerated cargo hold was packed with frozen beef from Australia. Batavian high society was beside itself with joy: Its members could eat as well in Java as they once had in Amsterdam.

northern slope [of Perboewatan] was covered with a dark gray ash layer, here and there showing a few bare tree stumps as meager relics of the impenetrable forests which not too long ago covered the island. Horrible was the view of that somber and empty landscape, which portrayed itself as a picture of total destruction rising from the sea, and from which, with incredible beauty and thundering power, rose a column of smoke."

The *Loudon*'s captain, T. H. Lindeman, steered the ship well away from the island. But he loaned a small boat to Schuurman, who landed at the northern end of Krakatoa along with the ship's engineer and a small party of curious daredevils. They struggled through tephra—volcanic ash—into which they sank up to their calves. The beach was covered with pumice.

The foolhardiness of the explorers knew no bounds. Knowing how dangerous and unpredictable it had to be, they climbed the crater and stared in amazement down into the deep, dish-shaped basin. Its bottom, Schuurman noted, was covered with a "dull, shiny crust," which occasionally emitted a rosy glow through which a powerful column of smoke escaped with what he then admitted was a truly frightening noise. They saw steam escaping from a number of cracks and gaps.

The men stayed for most of the day, burning the soles of their shoes, coughing and spluttering in the clouds of ash, and occasionally darting for shelter when the crater burped out a greater than usual bubble of smoke and sulfurous gas. Just after six o'clock the tropical darkness began to fall, and Captain Lindeman sounded the *Loudon*'s steam horn to urge everyone to get off the island. "We started our return trip to Batavia at 8 o'clock in the evening," Schuurman noted at the end of his official report, "thankful for the beauty and for a spectacle which made a deep impression on all, and an unforgettable one on most."

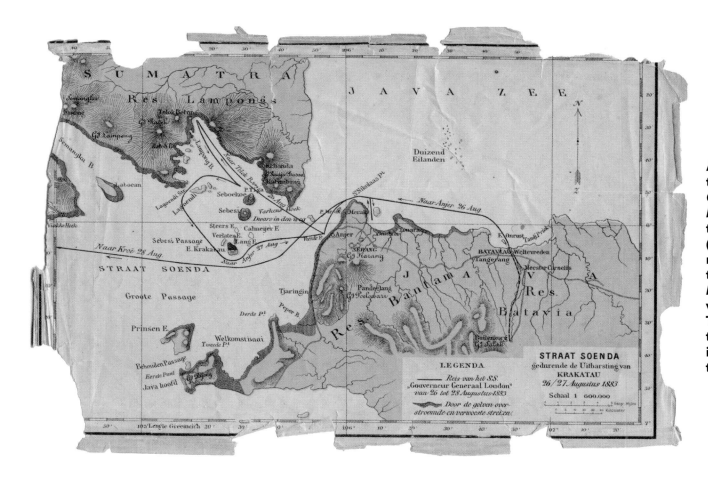

A Dutch map showing the route of the *Gouverneur-Generaal Loudon* from Batavia to Krakatoa (Krakatau on the map). Also shown are the routes of the *Loudon*'s later voyages that week. The shaded areas on the coastlines of the islands indicate where the tsunamis struck.

Two Javanese boys harvesting screwpines, known locally as pandan, in the Buitenzorg Botanical Garden. The tree is incredibly versatile, with its various parts used in housing, clothing, baskets and mats, cooking, medicine, as well as for religious purposes.

Island Deathwatch

During the next eight weeks, volcanic activity on Krakatoa became commonplace, like the equatorial heat and humidity. No one really gave it much thought. Some Batavians even made jokes about the rumblings and grumblings on the island. According to one observer, "visitors to Batavia, unless they had made inquiries, might have failed to hear of its existence at all." Henry Ogg Forbes, the Scottish explorer, ornithologist, botanist, and geologist who spent a good part of his career in the nearby islands of the Moluccas and New Guinea, later pleaded for information about this period of Krakatoa's life. He said that many of the ships' reports he had seen

Watching the Eruption, an illustration by F. H. Shell, depicts what it was like for ships carrying tourists who wished to see the eruptions on Krakatoa.

seemed to have been written "either with the mind bewildered and confused by the terrifying incidents amid which the officers found themselves, or from the after-recollection of the events, of which under such circumstances the important dry facts of time, place, and succession are liable to be unconsciously misstated."

One seemingly reliable report that did come to light—though half a century later—was from a young Liverpool seaman named R. J. Dalby. In June 1883 his ship stopped for a short stay at the west Java port of Anjer. Dalby was given shore leave and he took a canoe across the Sunda Strait to visit Krakatoa. In 1937 he was interviewed on a radio show and recalled that the view on all sides of the island was ". . . a real paradise, a profusion of vegetation rising from the seashore to the summit of hills several thousand feet high. I well remember one particular evening, just at the time when the land and sea breezes were at rest, the very atmosphere impressed one with a mystical awe. It was enhanced by the subtle scent of the spice trees, so plentiful on the island and, to crown it all, the sweet yet weird and melancholy chant of some natives, paddling their canoe close in to the dark shore. There were three of us in the boat, and we rested a long time trying to take in the strange grandeur of our surroundings; it was at this time that we noticed a long straight column of black smoke, going up from the peak of Krakatoa Island."

It's worth noting that Dalby's account contradicts Schuurman's report of Krakatoa being "bare and dry." Unfortunately, the answer for such a difference must remain a speculation. Was Dalby's recollection new evidence that by June the high peak of Rakata had joined the lowest one of Perboewatan in erupting? Certainly a second crater had opened up later on that month. After a stiff wind had died down on June 24, people on the Javan coast could see quite clearly that two separate columns of smoke were rising.

N E W S   B R I E F S

▲ Telegraph messages were sent one of two ways: by undersea cables or cables strung over land. Messages sent by the undersea cables were transmitted faster and were usually reserved for important or urgent messages, which were more expensive. For the important messages, an individual checked the box labeled "Via Eastern." These types of telegrams from Batavia would usually reach Amsterdam within three hours. If the message was sent routinely, it might take a week before the message arrived.

▲ R. D. M. Verbeek wrote the first major book about the eruption, *Krakatau*, which was published in 1886 by the Dutch Government Printing Office.

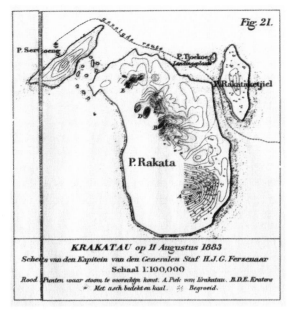

KRAKATAU op 11 Augustus 1883
Schets van den Kapitein van den Generalen Staf H.J.G. Ferzenaar
Schaal 1:100,000
Rood Punten waar stoom te voorschijn komt. A.Piek van Krakatau. B.D.E.Kraters
* Met asch bedekt en kaal. ፨ Begroeid.

Captain Ferzenaar's map of Krakatoa, drawn just sixteen days before the eruption

There were other observers during this period, but their accounts shed little light on the matter.

Mr. Beyerinck, the controller from Ketimbang who had first paddled to the island in May, returned to Krakatoa in July. He reported that he found two craters erupting, but his description is so confusing that it is impossible to know exactly which two craters he saw.

On August 11, 1883, a Dutch army captain named H. J. G. Ferzenaar, who had been ordered to prepare a survey of the island for the military topographic service, landed and spent two days there. He went alone. The local governor and other officials were too timid to accompany him. And with good reason.

Ferzenaar found all three craters erupting. In addition, he counted fourteen vents, or fumaroles, in the rocky surface from which grayish or pink smoke was rising.

He paddled his prahu around the eastern coast of Krakatoa, turned around the northern headland, passed on the outer side of the small sliver of an island on the northwest side—and then called it a day. Heavy smoke made visibility difficult; navigation, especially since the prahu did not have mechanical power, was exhausting. He drew a map that showed as much detail as possible, including the tiny spots and streaks of red from which the new eruptions were beginning.

This small map would have to do. He later wrote that any proper survey of the island had "to wait until later, because measuring there is still too dangerous; at least, I would not like to accept the responsibility of sending a surveyor."

As he sailed away from Krakatoa on August 12, Captain Ferzenaar could not know that he would be the last person to set foot on Krakatoa and that his map was the last record of the entire fifteen square miles of the tropical island.

Steam venting out of fumaroles on a volcano dome

The Circus Elephant

A very small circus elephant, said by his keeper, Miss Nanette Lochart, to be the smallest trained pachyderm in world history, was one of a hundred acts that made up John and Anna Wilson's Great World Circus. Everyone loved the little elephant, who arrived in Batavia on July 30, 1883. Children were captivated by the sight of the pachyderm juggling balls with his three-foot trunk or stepping gaily from tub to tub as he negotiated a little obstacle course.

But Miss Lochart began acting strangely. For reasons not explained, she decided that some of her fellow circus performers might try to harm the animal that was her only source of income. And so, midway through August, when the ash falls and thunderings and pillars of flame from Krakatoa were just beginning to be noticed once again in Batavia, Miss Lochart moved her little elephant into her room at the elegant Hotel des Indes. Without telling the hotel owner, M. Louis Cressonnier, she settled the animal down, said her good nights, and left for an evening with friends.

The elephant, denied the company of his mistress, clearly unaccustomed to the luxury and comfort on offer in the East's premier hotel, and perhaps—just perhaps—sensitive to vibrations caused by seismic activity one hundred miles west, promptly went berserk. He trampled all the furniture in Miss Lochart's room, smashing it to smithereens. He trumpeted. He roared. He stamped his feet. Guests thought the entire hotel was about to fall down. The police were called. Miss Lochart was found. She was told that she and her two-ton pet must leave the hotel at once.

No one guessed that the elephant's unusual behavior might be caused by something other than loneliness in unfamiliar surroundings.

NEWS BRIEFS

▲ The most famous attraction in the Great World Circus was John Holtum, the Cannonball King. Holtum was a thirty-eight-year-old Dane who had developed the skill of catching a cannonball fired at him from the far side of the circus ring. The first time he tried the stunt, the fifty-pound cannonball, flying at about one hundred miles an hour, tore off three fingers. Despite this, he persisted and became famous for his ability. By the time the circus arrived at Batavia in 1883, Holtum, who enjoyed challenging others to a cannonball catching contest, had bested 161 volunteers from Europe and the United States.

▲ Though there is no firm scientific evidence to support it, some geologists do feel it is at least reasonable to suppose that the subterranean shiftings and strainings that precede massive eruptions or earthquakes can be sensed by animals long before being experienced by man or his machines. A retired U.S. Geological Survey scientist living in the San Francisco area collected lost-pet advertisements in American newspapers and claimed to find a correlation, such that within two weeks of any rise in the number of missing animals, there was an earthquake nearby.

The Hotel des Indes

KRAKATOA DIES

NEWS BRIEFS

▲ Mr. Schuit, owner of the Anjer Hotel, was also an agent for Lloyd's of London, a premier society of insurance underwriters for ships. He sent a Via Eastern telegraph message to Lloyd's when he saw the eruption on Krakatoa because he knew it would affect the company's business. That message would be the first news to the world that something big was happening at Krakatoa.

▲ The Anjer Hotel had an excellent view of the harbor and Sunda Strait, and Schuit had a large brass telescope mounted under the hotel porch so he could watch and identify distant passing ships. Because wireless radio transmission had not yet been invented, Mr. Schuit would record their signal flag messages. He would look out for one particular arrangement of signal flags that read "ZD2." This was code that meant "Please report my passing to Lloyd's London."

Sunday, August 26, 1883

On Sunday, August 26, people on Java, Sumatra, and other islands in the Dutch East Indies colony were looking forward to the traditional day of rest.

In the west Java port of Anjer, European families were participating in a familiar Dutch ritual, the Sunday afternoon family walk. They sauntered along the broad seafront avenues, under groves of tamarind trees, passing and greeting local Javanese. And then, without warning, a loud sound came from somewhere west in the Sunda Strait.

The newly appointed telegraph master, Mr. Schruit, was resting on the veranda of the Anjer Hotel when he heard the first roar of an explosion. It was an extraordinary sound, far, far louder than anything he recalled from before. He looked sharply out to sea toward Krakatoa and saw, instantly, the unforgettable sight of a tremendous eruption. Billows of white smoke were tumbling up from one of its volcanoes—"as if thousands of white balloons had been released from the crater," he would later write.

The Anjer Hotel, owned by Mr. Schuit, where Mr. Schruit, the telegraph master, witnessed Krakatoa's eruption

This nineteenth-century drawing of Perboewatan's eruption was one of many compelling illustrations in the Royal Society's published study of Krakatoa's eruption. Today photographs, like the one at left, have largely replaced drawings to show the awesome power of volcanic eruptions.

Thick clouds of ash similar to the clouds that erupted from Krakatoa rise from this more recent volcano in Nicaragua.

And whatever was happening on Krakatoa was also having an immediate effect on the waters of Sunda Strait. The seawater was rising and falling, strongly, irregularly, in bursts of sudden up-and-down movements. It seemed unnatural and sinister.

Mr. Schruit and his deputy, who was strolling on the beach when the eruption happened, ran to the small white stone building that was the Anjer telegraph office. As they hurried, an enormous cloud from the volcano began to drift down on the area. Within a few minutes all Anjer was covered in dust and cloud.

Later some would say the cloud was black. Others, like Schruit, were equally certain that it was white. One of the pilots who helped guide ships through the busy strait, Mr. de Vries, swore it alternated from white to black. The rapidly expanding cloud was so dense that it soon blotted out the sun. Though it was the middle of the afternoon, Anjer was plunged into the darkness of midnight. Mr. Schruit and his deputy had to light lanterns in order to send their first message to Batavia about a hundred miles east. At two p.m. they tapped out the urgent message that Krakatoa was "vomiting fire and smoke." The telegraph also noted the darkness in Anjer; it was impossible to see one's hand before one's eyes. It concluded with a request for instructions.

The response from Batavia was swift. Headquarters was aware that something extraordinary was taking place. Schruit and his deputy were told to keep sending updates. For the next six hours they gave a moment-by-moment chronicle in the staccato language of the telegraph: "Detonations increasing in loudness." "Hails of pumice." "Rain of coarse ash." "First flooding." "Vessels breaking loose in harbor." "Unusual darkness." "Gathering gloom."

Meanwhile in Batavia, Dr. J. P. van der Stok, whose wife had lost her Delft dinner plate, checked his watch at the very moment he heard the first loud rumblings. He dashed from his house to the observatory and wrote the

A cloud of steam spreads out in the sky over the volcano Augustine. In August 1883, a similar, though thicker, cloud filled with ash rose over Krakatoa and spread over the region. The cloud was so thick and dense it completely blocked out sunlight, turning day to night.

time in the official log. Van der Stok had recorded for posterity the precise time of the beginning of the final phase in the life of Krakatoa: 1:06 p.m.

At five o'clock Sunday evening, when twilight was normally an hour away, it was nearly totally dark up and down the entire west coast of Java and was starting to become dark at Batavia. The air was hot and poisonous, filled with ash, grit and sulfur. Enormous chunks of rock were raining down from the sky. Three ships, caught in the strait, were showered by the hot cascade of pumice hurled out of Krakatoa. One of them, the *Loudon*, unable to reach safety at Telok Betong, anchored in Lampong Bay, hoping to ride out the surging sea.

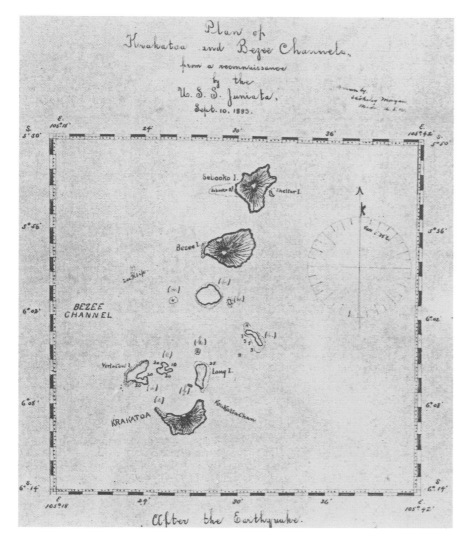

The first post-eruption map of Krakatoa was drawn less than a month later, on September 10, 1883, by a crew member of the USS *Juniata*. The sloop, under the command of Commodore George Dewey, was on a three-year voyage around the world. During the trip it stopped at Batavia.

▲ Captain Sampson of the British ship *Norham Castle* anchored his vessel off the coast of Sumatra to wait out the rough seas caused by events at Krakatoa. He recorded events in his official log: "I am writing this blind in pitch darkness. We are under a continual rain of pumice-stone and dust. So violent are the explosions that the ear-drums of over half my crew have been shattered. My last thoughts are with my dear wife. I am convinced that the Day of Judgment has come." But Captain Sampson and his ship survived.

Monday, August 27, 1883

On the morning of Monday, August 27, like the tolling of a bell of doom, four explosions announced the final countdown of Krakatoa's existence. The first occurred at 5:30 a.m. The second came at 6:15 a.m. Then, a little more than two hours later, at 8:20 a.m., a third, quite terrible explosion was felt in Batavia.

The fourth—and what would be the most violent explosion ever recorded and experienced by modern man—occurred at 10:02 a.m. It could be heard thousands of miles away! But by then few people were left to hear the sound in the coastal towns of Java and Sumatra that bordered the Sunda Strait. Almost everyone in them had been killed by the gigantic tsunamis caused by Krakatoa's explosions.

An illustration of one of the giant tsunamis created by Krakatoa's eruption and that struck the town of Anjer, Java

▲ When Krakatoa annihilated itself, an estimated six cubic miles of rock had been blasted out of existence.

▲ Most people killed in volcanic eruptions die as result of suffocation from poisonous gas, or being buried by swift-moving pyroclastic flows—dense clouds composed of a mixture of hot ashes, lava fragments, and gases. Sometimes they are buried by mud slides. What made the Krakatoa deaths exceptional was that there were so many and that most happened because of tsunamis.

▲ Though standardized time zones for the world had been proposed in 1876, they had still not been officially accepted as late as 1884. Therefore, administrators in the Dutch East Indies established time in their own districts. Each administrator would set the official watch according to when the sun rose and set and reached its noontime peak in his particular district. As a result, there are a wide variety of local time records in the Dutch East Indies for the events that occurred on August 27.

A boy kneels before a gigantic piece of coral weighing several tons that rests where the Anjer post office once stood. The coral was flung ashore by Krakatoa's eruption.

Impact Near . . .

The death throes of Krakatoa lasted from 1:06 p.m. Sunday to 10:02 a.m. Monday—exactly twenty hours and fifty-six minutes. But its effect on the world continued for more than a year. Five days after Krakatoa had exploded, Alexander Patrick Cameron, the British consul in Batavia, wrote the head of the Foreign Office, in London: ". . . the whole of the southeastern coast of Sumatra must have suffered severely from the effects of the sudden influx of the sea, and thousands of natives inhabiting the villages on the coast must have almost certainly perished.

"The west coast of Java from Merak to Tjeringin [has] been laid waste. Anjer . . . a thriving town of several thousand inhabitants (natives), no longer exists, its former site now being a swamp.

"The lighthouse at Anjer (Java's Fourth Point) has also been much damaged.

". . . in the district of Tjeringin alone on the southeast coast of Java it is reported that no less than ten thousand persons have lost their lives."

In the aftermath of Krakatoa's eruption, 165 villages were devastated, an estimated 36,417 people died, and uncountable thousands were injured. Almost all of them were victims not of the eruption directly but of the immense sea waves, or tsunamis, that were propelled outward from the volcano by the last explosions.

Because of the number of massive and highly destructive sea waves it produced, Krakatoa is unique. Careful study of the records for the last two and a half centuries has come up with a total of some ninety tsunamis for which volcanoes alone can be held responsible—and the greatest of these by far were from the 1883 eruption of Krakatoa. About a thousand people were killed by heat from fiery ash and pumice and scalding-hot gases of the volcano. More than thirty-five thousand were killed by the several gigantic waves caused by the explosion.

Which of the waves that Monday killed the vast majority of those who were lost? Eyewitness accounts do not agree. An elderly Dutch pilot in Anjer believed the first wave was the worst. He later wrote, "As I clung to the palm tree . . . there floated past the dead bodies of many a friend and neighbour. Only a mere handful of the population escaped. Houses and trees were completely destroyed, and scarcely a trace remains of where the once busy, thriving town originally stood."

A second great wave, what observers called a "giant black wall of water," roared into the town of Telok Betong on Sumatra. R. A. van Sandick, a passenger aboard the *Loudon* in Lampong Bay, was an eyewitness to what happened next. He later wrote that a series of waves, traveling at tremendous speed sometime between 7:30 and 8:30 a.m. ". . . destroyed all of Telok Betong before our eyes. The light tower could be seen to tumble, the houses disappeared... everything had become sea in front of our eyes, where a few minutes before Telok Betong beach had been. The impressiveness of this scene is difficult to describe."

This twisted metal wreckage in the ruined coastal town of Merak on Java is evidence of the powerful destructive force of the tsunamis that swept the islands bordering the Sunda Strait.

On December 12, 1992, a smaller tsunami struck the Indonesian island of Flores, about 1,120 miles east of Jakarta, and stripped the coastline of vegetation and buildings up to about three hundred feet inland.

An etching of the steamship *Berouw* resting almost intact across the Koeripan River in Sumatra and more than two miles inland from its mooring in Telok Betong harbor

Eleven years later, an 1894 photo shows that only the *Berouw*'s boiler remains as a memento of how far the tsunami reached.

One tsunami wave, estimated to be 135 feet high, struck Merak at 9:00 a.m., destroyed stone buildings that stood on top of a 115-foot-high hill, and drowned all but two of the town's 2,700 inhabitants.

Then, at 10:30 a.m., after the fourth and largest explosion had occurred, another colossal wave, traveling at about sixty miles an hour, smashed onto the shores of Java and Sumatra. Its impact, reportedly, ". . . carried away the remaining portions of the towns of Tjiringin, Merak and Telok Betong, as well as many other hamlets and villages near the shore."

One of the most astonishing stories during the catastrophe is that of the *Berouw*. Unable to dock at Telok Betong because of the rough seas, the ship managed to ride out the chaotic conditions from Sunday through early Monday. But then disaster struck. The first huge tsunami wave lifted the hapless ship up, snapping the mooring lines that were attached to a buoy. The *Berouw* was transported high on the crest of a mighty wall of green water. She was swept westward for a quarter of a mile until, as the wave broke, she was dropped onto shore, at the mouth of the Koeripan River. About three hours later, another great wave smashed onto the shore. Once again the *Berouw* was lifted high and carried westward a further two miles upriver. When the tsunami wave collapsed, the *Berouw* landed astride the Koeripan River, forming a bridge, sixty feet above sea level. Though the twenty-eight crew members were dead, the ship itself had suffered only minor damage.

The same could not be said for the towns along the surrounding coasts of Java and Sumatra—they were ruined beyond belief. Thousands upon thousands of people were crushed, drowned, or never to be found again.

As the few remaining survivors took stock of the enormity of what they had lost, those who were able looked out over the Sunda Strait in the direction of the source of the destruction. But, instead of seeing Krakatoa, they saw something even more astonishing—Krakatoa was gone!

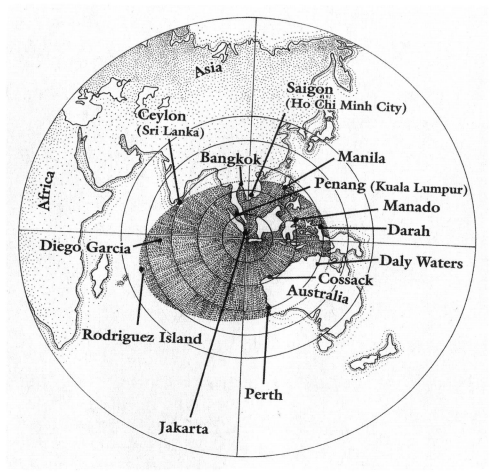

A chart showing how far the sound of Krakatoa's explosion traveled

NEWS BRIEFS

▲ The most common recorded description of Krakatoa's explosions was "cannon fire." This was mentioned by people in the distant island of Diego Garcia as well as cattle ranchers in western Australia.

▲ According to legend, a group of Dayak tribesmen on the island of Borneo had recently murdered a local official, eaten part of his body, and shrunk his head as a keepsake. When hearing the sounds of Krakatoa's self-destruction, they assumed it was the authorities come to take revenge for the murder and fled deep into the jungle.

. . . And Impact Far

Rodriguez Island, located in the western half of the Indian Ocean, was at the time a remote, idyllic tropical island belonging to Great Britain. It was 2,968 miles east of Krakatoa. The nearest large landmass was the island of Madagascar, more than one thousand miles farther west. In 1881 only five thousand people lived there, farming and fishing. Their only contact with the outside world was irregular visits by sailing ships chartered to bring mail, goods, and the occasional government official or tourist. It was a paradise where not much happened.

That changed in August 1883.

Fine volcanic ash suspended in the air causes brilliant atmospheric conditions like this sunset over the Alaskan volcano Augustine in February 2006. Ash from Krakatoa created spectacular sunsets around the world.

In his monthly official report, Chief of Police James Wallis noted that the weather on August 26 was stormy, with heavy rain and rough seas. He also wrote that during the night of August 26–27 for three to four hours he heard in the east what sounded like the repeated firing of cannons.

But police chief Wallis did not hear the sound of cannons that night. What he heard was the sound of Krakatoa destroying itself. It was as if a sound originating in Baltimore was heard by someone in San Francisco.

Krakatoa's tsunamis in the Dutch East Indies reached far and wide. With no large landmass to hinder or stop them, the tsunamis traveled west across the Indian Ocean. A series of fourteen waves, some as high as twelve feet and traveling 370 miles an hour, struck the shores of the island of Ceylon (Sri Lanka), killing one woman in the southeastern port city of Panama and smashing boats along the coast. Four-foot-high waves touched the shore of South Africa. The surge of ocean waves did not stop but continued up the coast of Africa to Europe. At Socoa, a small French harbor town on the Atlantic coast near Spain, tide gauges recorded seven three-inch-high surges. Socoa is 10,729 nautical miles from Krakatoa! The surge continued northward, entering the English Channel, more than 11,000 miles from its point of origin, before finally reaching its limit, causing just a slight ripple in the tide chart records at Cherbourg and Le Havre in France and Devonport on the coast of England.

Dust of all grades and compositions was thrown into the air by the eruption. Much of it was too heavy to remain in the air for long. Ash rained down on ships (one as far as 3,700 miles from Krakatoa). It also coated the land with layer upon layer of what was most often described as "cement."

The finest dust particles were thrown up to thirty miles into the air. At that distance, in the different levels of the stratosphere and troposphere, such dust particles could remain aloft for months or years. And because they refracted and filtered sunlight, people around the world for months to come saw some of the most spectacular and colorful sunsets ever.

News of Krakatoa's eruption and the subsequent fiery sunsets reportedly greatly upset painter Edvard Munch and were the inspiration for his famous painting *The Scream*.

▲ Under the impact of Krakatoa's explosion, 13 percent of the earth's surface vibrated audibly. The millions who heard the noise were stunned when they were told its source.

▲ A major scientific investigation into the events surrounding the eruption at Krakatoa was soon launched. It is a measure of how much the British and its Royal Society were held in respect that though Krakatoa was in a territory that belonged to the Dutch government, the leading scientific investigation into the events of the eruption was led by and composed of a group of entirely British experts.

▲ For Reuters, the real value of the telegraph was speed. To beat the competition and be the first to have a scoop on the news was all-important. For example, to get news from Paris to Brussels before the telegraph link had been completed, Reuters had used special carrier pigeons.

▲ Newspapers and magazines were the main sources of information during the nineteenth century.

A map showing part of the worldwide network of telegraph connections used by Reuters

Reuters Reports

That Krakatoa became famous enough to achieve a status that endures to this day is based in large part upon one of the great business creations of that period: the news agency. Reuters, based in London, was the first. It was founded by Julius Reuter, a visionary German-Jewish businessman who began his career as a small-time newspaper publisher in Paris in the mid 1800s. When the telegraph was invented in the 1840s, Reuter immediately knew it was a valuable tool. He saw that companies, particularly newspapers, would be willing to pay for news and its fast delivery.

His news service began full-scale operation on October 8, 1858, and within two years he had a hundred correspondents worldwide. By 1883, Reuters was the biggest international news agency in the world with an unmatched reputation for speed and reliability.

Reuters had an office in Batavia and employed what is known as a stringer, a freelance writer who submitted suitable local news stories to the agency. In 1883 Reuters' stringer in Batavia was W. Brewer. He would become the envy of journalists everywhere by being in the right place at the right time.

Thanks to Reuters, reports filed by Mr. Brewer began appearing in major newspapers around the world. People were fascinated by events in what was for most an unknown group of islands.

It's easy to see why. News of Krakatoa's explosion became the first-ever story about a truly enormous natural event that was told as the events unfolded. Part of the planet's fabric had been ripped asunder, and the story began within hours of its occurrence, not weeks or months after the fact. This immediacy, combined with the extraordinary, jaw-dropping scope of the catastrophe, ensured that Krakatoa would become part of the cultural memory of modern mankind.

This is *Earthrise*, the photo taken by astronaut William Anders on December 24, 1968, during the *Apollo 8* mission that circled the moon. The image, showing Earth as a tiny blue globe in the vastness of space, had enormous emotional impact. Like the 1883 explosion at Krakatoa, it made people aware of how small and fragile Earth is.

Shock Waves

One of the many striking things about the late nineteenth century was the widespread availability of affordable and accurate instruments that measured and recorded the weather. Many middle-class homes, particularly in England, contained barometers, recording thermometers, sun gauges, and rain gauges. As a result there was an army of amateur meteorologists.

The most costly and sophisticated of these instruments was the recording barograph. With an ink trace on a sheet of graph paper wrapped around a clockwork-driven drum, it recorded the slight hourly variations in atmospheric pressure over the week that it took for the drum to rotate a single time.

When these recording papers were changed after Krakatoa erupted, monitors throughout the world noticed something quite unusual had happened in the atmosphere on Monday, August 27. Instead of a smooth or lazily curving line of ink from the recording pen, there was an abrupt and very sharp up-and-down series of oscillations on the paper chart.

It seemed as though there had been the quite impossible occurrence of an earthquake in the air.

It took only hours of excited discussion between official meteorologists and weather-fascinated amateurs to conclude that the unusual atmospheric condition their barographs had recorded was related to Krakatoa.

From locations around the world close examination of the graphs confirmed the astonishing fact: The shock wave did not sweep across the globe only once that day; it did so seven times.

For the first time people saw that a natural event occurring in one corner of the planet had effects that spread over the entire world. The world was now suddenly seen to be much more than an immense collection of unrelated peoples and isolated happenings.

THE ILLUSTRATED LONDON NEWS.

No. 2316.—VOL. LXXXIII.

SATURDAY, SEPTEMBER 8, 1883.

WITH TWO SUPPLEMENTS

SIXPENCE.
By Post, 6½d.

ISLAND OF KRAKATOA, IN THE STRAITS OF SUNDA, THE CENTRE OF THE LATE VOLCANIC ERUPTION, SAID TO HAVE DISAPPEARED.

EAST COAST AND ISLANDS OF THE STRAITS OF SUNDA, WITH ANJER, A PORT OF JAVA.

THE STRAITS OF SUNDA, AS SEEN AFTER LEAVING ANJER.

THE VOLCANIC ERUPTION IN THE STRAITS OF SUNDA.

Krakatoa's eruption was a major topic of conversation around the world for weeks. *The Illustrated London News* was one of countless newspapers and magazines that ran stories about the event.

▲ Pumice is one of the better-known rocks produced by volcanoes. Its low density is caused by gas bubbles trapped inside the molten rock before it solidifies, which is why it floats. Its abrasive ability makes it useful for cleaning purposes. It is also the ingredient used by the makers of distressed jeans to whiten and age the fabric.

▲ In early 1884, on the west coast of the island of Kosrae, in what is now Pacific Micronesia, huge plates of pumice sixteen inches thick were hauled from the beach. They were covered with barnacles, and many contained the roots of huge trees, with extra pumice lumps caught up in their roots, helping them stay afloat. These trees, torn up and floating three thousand miles to the east, were presumably parts of Krakatoa's old forests.

▲ The crew of the British ship *Bay of Naples* claimed that when the ship was 120 miles from Java it encountered carcasses of numerous animals, including tigers, and about 150 human corpses as well as enormous tree trunks.

Pumice on the beach of Anak Krakatau

Death Rafts

Shock waves and dust particles traveled hundreds of miles an hour. The immense rafts of floating pumice that splashed into the seas around Krakatoa drifted away at the leisurely pace of just a half mile an hour. As they moved, the pumice rafts absorbed the unidentifiable remains of some of the unfortunate thousands of Javanese and Sumatrans, Dutchmen and Chinese, and other peoples who had perished.

The crews of ships moving through fields of pumice were struck by the peculiar sound of the bow slicing through the rock. There was no real noise, "just a soft sort of crushing sound," wrote one sailor. A crewman on the vessel *Samoa* wrote of the nightmarish unreality of such encounters in the Sunda Strait: "For two days after passing Anjer we passed through masses of dead bodies, hundreds and hundreds of them striking the ships on both sides—groups of 50 and 100 all packed together, most of them naked. We passed a great deal of wreckage, but of course we cannot tell if any vessels were lost. We also passed bedding chests and a number of white bodies, all dressed like sailors, with sheath knives on them. For ten days, we went through fields of pumice stone."

Some large pieces of pumice would reach the southeast coast of Africa more than a year after Krakatoa's destruction.

After the eruption, the British Royal Society made appeals for information in newspapers throughout the world as part of its effort to gather as much information as possible about Krakatoa. A headmistress of a mission school in Zanzibar, now a part of Tanzania, wrote that about the third week in July 1884 there was a large quantity of human skulls and bones stripped of all flesh scattered "all along the beach at high water-mark."

Stories of Sunda Strait filled with corpses swept to sea by the tsunamis inspired the horror of this drawing of what ships actually experienced.

Weather Changes

The British Royal Society's *The Eruption of Krakatoa and Subsequent Phenomena* was published in 1888. Two-thirds of the society's 494-page report is devoted to unusual atmospheric events around the world.

There were four main kinds of phenomena attributed to dust and ash. There were 1) the sunsets, 2) the vivid and highly unusual colorations of the moon (often blue, sometimes green), 3) the occasional colorations of the sun, and very rarely, colorations of some of the larger planets, and 4) whitish solar coronas frequently seen just before sunset, and monstrously flaming afterglows.

A pattern also emerged from the Royal Society's catalog of observations. There could be no doubt that the immense cloud of stratospheric ash that spread out from Krakatoa wound itself around the planet in a westerly direction, as one might expect, with the world turning eastward underneath. It spread both northward and southward.

Traveling at about 73 miles per hour, the dust began reaching New York state in November, creating spectacular red sunsets. In fact, the sunsets were so striking and unusual that the Poughkeepsie Fire Department was fooled into thinking that a fire had broken out. Only after racing to the Hudson River did they sheepishly discover that the bright red glow in the sky was caused by something in the atmosphere and not by flames from burning buildings.

The dust had another effect on the planet. The day after the explosion, Batavians noticed that the weather had gotten noticeably colder. Dense clouds as much as a hundred and fifty miles in diameter hung above the city for days, preventing sunlight from penetrating. When they checked their thermometers, they discovered that the temperature was sixty-five degrees Fahrenheit, fifteen degrees lower than normal.

NEWS BRIEFS

▲ Unfortunately, in an amazing oversight, the Royal Society completely neglected to list temperature records in its study. The first real study of the climate change did not happen until 1913. A second was made in 1982. Both found that the temperature around the world had dropped an average of one degree Fahrenheit.

▲ The spectacular sunsets inspired artists all over the world. One of them was landscape artist Frederic Edwin Church. His *Sunset over the Ice on Chaumont Bay, Lake Ontario*, painted on December 28, 1883, is believed to be an artistic recording of a spectacular sunset caused by dust particles from Krakatoa.

▲ William Ascroft, a London artist, was so inspired by the sunsets he saw that he painted more than 533 watercolors of them. Five hundred of the paintings were later displayed in an exhibition in a museum in South Kensington.

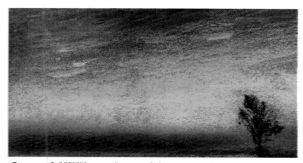

One of William Ascroft's sunsets

▲ The heavier dust thrown into the air began to settle within two weeks. Two ships, the *Brani* and the *British Empire*, sailing in the Indian Ocean about two thousand miles from Krakatoa found themselves encountering a slow rain of white ash that one member of the crew said "looked like Portland cement." Another ship, the *Scotia*, encountered falling dust as far away as the Horn of Africa, 3,700 miles from Krakatoa.

LIFE RETURNS

Rakata

Referred to as Krakatoa in the popular press, Krakatau resumed its proper spelling once public interest had passed. Amazingly a piece of it survived the destruction: the southern part containing the volcano Rakata. Seared and scarred, from a distance it appeared that Rakata, as the island fragment was later called, had been stripped of all life.

One of the many questions following the eruption was the condition of Rakata and how and in what form life would return to its blasted surface. Scientists from around the world packed their bags and instruments and notebooks and headed for the Sunda Strait. They knew that nature had handed them the opportunity of a lifetime. It was frustrating that there were no accurate records of life that existed on Krakatau before August 27. All that could be said with certainty was that the island had been covered with a snail-rich, orchid-rich, pepper-infested, and grass-floored tropical rain forest, more or less similar to that found in Sumatra.

One biologist wrote in his journal that it would "be very interesting to follow step-by-step the progress of the development of new life on this land now dead but which, in a few years, thanks to the intense heat of the sun and the abundance of equatorial rains, will surely have been recovered in its green mantle."

Rogier Verbeek was the first on Rakata, in October, just six weeks after the eruption. As it turned out, he had arrived too soon. When he stepped onto the dusty shore, the island's surface was still almost too hot to touch, and mud flows were still pouring from the lava cliffs. He could see no evidence that anything living existed on the island.

The first scientist to discover life on what remained of Krakatau was the Belgian biologist Edmond Cotteau, part of a scientific expedition sponsored by the French government. When the expedition landed in May 1884, it encountered the same devastation witnessed by Dr. Verbeek. As they began their exploration, they had to avoid the dangers of cliff erosion—

Three well-to-do Dutch people enjoying a day at Buitenzorg

NEWS BRIEFS

▲ A controversy soon arose regarding the question of whether or not any life on Rakata survived the eruption. Some scientists believed no life, not even small plants, could have survived. Others claimed that it was possible, even probable, for some small plant forms to have survived. The controversy became so strong in the botanic community that it was given a name: the Krakatau problem.

▲ Cornelius Andries Backer, the Botanist with Special Responsibility for the Flora of Java at the Buitenzorg Botanical Gardens, was the central figure in the Krakatau problem controversy. He visited Rakata in 1906. In his report of his visit, he wrote, ". . . it is clear that no vestige of the flora would have been able to exist after the cataclysm. The most persistent seed and the most protected rhizome must have perished." Twenty-two years after the eruption, evidence appeared of a large cycad, a plant that looks like a cross between a palm and a fern, that appeared too big for one to have grown after the eruption. This evidence caused Backer to think that perhaps some life did survive, and he wound up completely changing his mind.

▲ In 1917, Johann Handle, a German, landed on the southern end of Rakata with his family and servants and announced he was going to make a living as a pumice collector. Unfortunately, the boat that carried them to Rakata also contained rats, which soon established themselves on the island.

rocks and boulders were constantly rolling down the steep cliff sides.

Cotteau was walking south on the beach when he spotted something moving on the rocks. With growing excitement, he discovered a small spider spinning a web. Within months, more and more life—plant and animal—would be seen on Rakata.

About a year after the explosion, crews of passing ships commented that they thought they saw patches of green plant life. In June 1886, a new expedition visited the island for four days. No fewer than fifteen flowering plants and shrubs were counted. For the most part these were beach plants, probably washed ashore from other islands. There were also two types of moss and eleven species of ferns. Some surfaces of the island were covered in a blue-green algae.

When another expedition arrived in 1887, the scientists discovered dense fields of grasses so tall that a person could hide in them. In addition there was wild sugarcane, creepers, hibiscus, orchids, a small assortment of trees, and more species of ferns.

By 1906 plant life had further spread across the island, and the trees were maturing. Animal life was abundant. Scientists discovered red and black ants and carpenter bees. There were colorful butterflies, earthworms, and such birds as the kingfishers, nightjars, green pigeons, wood swallows, bulbuls, and orioles. Some visitors even reported seeing a monitor lizard.

In just twenty years, Rakata was lush with new life.

Life returns to Rakata.

Rising Up

On June 27, 1927, some fishermen were hauling up their nets near Rakata when, with a great roaring and rumbling, a clump of enormous gas bubbles suddenly broke the surface of the sea around them. Frightened, they quickly sailed away. Later, in telling their stories to government officials, they gave their location as a point more or less above where Danan, the middle of the three Krakatau peaks, had once been. The bubbles were the first indication that a new volcano was building itself up from the sea floor.

Soon the bubbles became a steady stream that lasted for several weeks. Impressive fountains, some 120 feet high and composed of black froth, steam, ash, and chunks of pumice, followed. Then came a series of great domes of water—each a half-mile across—rising out of the sea as if being pushed up by something far below. What happened next was even more bizarre—jets of flame began to erupt from the water's surface. Observers had the impression that the water itself was on fire.

Six months later, on January 26, 1928, molten rock, ash, and lava broke the surface, creating what looked like a sand dune 500 feet long and ten feet high. A Russian geophysicist named W. A. Petroeschevsky, there to study the region in the wake of the eruption, saw the birth of this new island and named it Anak Krakatau—son of Krakatau.

New marine volcanoes more often than not die quickly. After a week the pounding waves of Sunda Strait wore away the small hump of land. All that was visible by mid-February was a patch of muddy-colored water, occasionally pierced by a funnel cloud of smoke, steam, ash, and every so often, by small pellets of hot lava.

Some months later, eruptions from two separate points created a pair of cones that rose seventy feet and were joined to each other by a slender spit of land. But when the volcanic activity stopped, the pounding waves eroded the new land and the small island disappeared beneath the sea.

For the next three years volcano and sea seemed to battle each other, with the volcano emerging in a cloud of steam and smoke only to have the waves and tides smash the lava crust to rubble and wash the remains away.

Sometimes it was not just the waves that did the destroying. In early August 1930, Anak Krakatau made a third attempt to rise above the surface, only to blow itself to pieces shortly after the lava broke the surface.

On August 11, 1930, Anak Krakatau emerged a fourth time—as a ring-shaped island that looked like a black doughnut. This time the island would not collapse beneath the sea. Instead, it would grow. By the end of the year, the mound of hot rock and ash was half a mile long and twenty feet above sea level at its highest point.

NEWS BRIEFS

▲ On February 3, 1928, during a twenty-four-hour period, an astonishing 11,791 volcanic explosions at Anak Krakatau were counted by scientists. Then, during another twenty-four-hour period on June 25, 1928, another 14,269 eruptions were counted—an average of ten eruptions every minute.

▲ Two days later after Anak Krakatau appeared for the fourth time, it seemed the island would once again destroy itself. Hot lava and gas combined with the cold seawater to create a phreatomagmatic eruption that blasted a huge amount of volcanic material about a mile straight up. This time, though, when the volcanic matter fell back it created a foundation of sorts that successive eruptions built upon.

▲ Phreatomagmatic eruptions are distinctive because the shape of the explosion resembles a gigantic rooster's tail.

Two photographs of Anak Krakatau explosively emerging from the sea in 1928

Though plant life has returned to Rakata, this 1924 photograph reveals that some raw scars from the 1883 eruption remain.

This 2006 photo shows lush plant life has taken full root on Rakata.

An Island Grows

Once it appeared that the fourth version of Anak Krakatau would not sink back beneath the sea like the three earlier ones, scientists had the rare opportunity to answer the fascinating question of how life begins and grows. They began to visit the island in droves. One of the first was William Syer Bristowe, a famous English arachnologist, who had already studied spider species on Rakata. Very quickly he discovered a beetle, a mosquito, some ants—and three species of spider.

In November 1931, fifteen months after Anak Krakatau broke the surface of the Sunda Strait, scientists visiting the northern coast of the island discovered it was littered with floating tree stumps, bamboo stems, roots, and decaying fruit. Eighteen seeds were discovered, ten of which had already taken root. In another visit a short time later, four more plant species were discovered to have taken root. And the variety of life on the island included moths, fungi, and some migratory birds.

In 1950 Anak Krakatau was a mile long and a half mile wide, with a five-hundred-foot-tall mountain, filled with a growing variety of plants and small animals. But a catastrophic eruption that year destroyed them. This pattern of life destroyed by volcanic eruption would occur three more times on Anak Krakatau, the last happening in 1953.

The geological makeup of the island began to change in the 1960s. Lava flows, previously unknown to occur in the region, began to cascade from the crater. Today about half the island is covered by black lava.

By 2000 the island's double-cratered volcano had reached the height of 1,500 feet above sea level. And because the volcano remains active, Anak Krakatau continues to grow.

A young Anak Krakatau

▲ Bristowe once calculated that the weight of insects eaten by British spiders in an average year was greater than the total weight of all the people living in Great Britain.

The constant volcanic activity on Anak Krakatau is causing the island to grow at a steady rate of five inches a week.

▲ Surprisingly, Anak Krakatau was largely left alone and neglected by scientists for twenty-five years. So many of the different stages of the growth and development of life on the island have not been recorded.

▲ Ian Thornton, an Australian biologist, created a simple experiment to see how rapidly insect life arrives on one of the seemingly barren lava flows on Anak Krakatau. He places plastic containers filled with seawater on top of the flows and then waits to see how many airborne spiders and insects they might catch. In one ten-day period, the containers captured seventy-two different species, including wasps, earwigs, moths, and beetles.

Members of an expedition visiting the crater of Anak Krakatau in 1951

Krakatau Today

About 150 species of plant now inhabit Anak Krakatau, living beside a volcano that is continuously pouring out ash and lava. Once the plants got established, providing seeds, fruit, shade, and moisture, and once insect colonies became varied and abundant, birds, lizards, and other animals came and stayed. These plants and animals are distinctly different from life on the nearby Rakata and Sertung and Panjang islands.

The first step in protecting all four islands was made in July 1919, when the Dutch government designated Anak Krakatau and part of Rakata as a national monument. In 1925 the Ujung Kulon Reserve, now the Ujung Kulon National Park, was expanded to include the rest of Rakata as well as Sertung and Panjang islands.

**A lava bomb
on Anak Krakatau**

NEWS BRIEFS

▲ The dangers of sailing in the Sunda Strait were underscored in 1985 when two twenty-seven-year-old California women, Rickey Berkowitz and Judy Schwartz, failed in an attempt to reach Krakatau. They found themselves drifting for three weeks in their leaky open boat, surviving on a diet of peanuts, rainwater, and toothpaste.

▲ Ujung Kulon National Park was declared a UNESCO World Heritage Site in 1992 because it has the largest remaining lowland rain forest in Java and is home to the rare one-horned Java rhinoceros.

▲ Ships passing through the Sunda Strait keep a close eye on the smoke rising from Anak Krakatau's peak. White smoke is a sign that everything is normal on the volcano. It's a sign of danger if the smoke fills with volcanic debris and turns gray. That means the volcano will explode soon.

A monitoring station on Anak Krakatau

Most of the western and northern shores of Anak Krakatau show no signs of life and are made of dark gray lava flows, with more recent lava being a paler shade. In contrast, the east side of the island is a lush, tropical wonderland, home to a wide variety of butterflies, birds, geckos, rats, and other animals, including monitor lizards.

But the image of paradise is an illusion. Large rocks and lava bombs—hundreds of them, some clearly weighing several tons—from recent eruptions are scattered along the volcano's slopes, silent evidence that the island is a dangerous place. Despite the potential for danger, and reminiscent of the voyage of the *Loudon*, the island has become a popular destination for tourists.

The most dangerous active volcanoes are those that store up their energy, only releasing it in one cataclysmic explosion like the one that happened on August 27, 1883. As long as Anak Krakatau continues to expel steam and debris, there is relatively little to fear. But the peculiar tectonics of Java and Sumatra make it certain that Anak Krakatau will at some point in the future catastrophically explode as Krakatau did.

Meanwhile, in the small town of Carita located on Java's west coast, there are some small, undistinguished wooden buildings painted in yellow and sitting on a low hill. The buildings are the field station of the Krakatau Volcanic Observatory. In one room is an old seismic sensor that measures vibrations coming from Anak Krakatau. And on the island itself, the Indonesian government has set up additional seismic monitors.

When Anak Krakatau decides to release its fury, these instruments will be there to warn the world and, like their nineteenth-century predecessors, record the consequences.

The eerie landscape near the summit of the cone of Anak Krakatau

alkaline metals: metals that are reactive and form basic oxides that when combined with water form comparatively insoluble oxides. The group includes magnesium, calcium, barium, and radium.

archipelago: a group of islands usually arranged in a long line

basalt: a dark, black volcanic rock that has low viscosity, allowing it to flow quickly when molten.

caldera: a very large, usually circular depression at the summit of a volcano formed when magma is withdrawn or erupted from a shallow underground magma reservoir. Calderas are different from craters, which are smaller circular depressions created primarily by explosive excavation of rock during eruptions.

Anak Krakatau today

consul: an official appointed by a government to live in a foreign city and protect and promote the government's citizens and interests there.

extinct volcano: a volcano that has not had an eruption in recorded history.

freelancer: someone who is not permanently employed by one company and does work for a variety of employers.

fumaroles: vents from which volcanic gas escapes into the atmosphere.

geology: the science that deals with the earth's physical structure and substance, its history, and the processes that act on it.

governor-general: the title in a monarchy of the most important government official in a territory the country possesses and who represents the royal government.

lava: hot molten or semifluid rock—magma—erupted from a volcano.

lithosphere: the rigid outer part of the earth, consisting of the crust and upper mantle.

log: sometimes called log book. An official record of events during the voyage of a ship or airplane, and a regular or systematic record of incidents or observations.

magma: hot fluid or semifluid material below or within the earth's crust from which lava and other igneous rock are formed by cooling.

mantle: the region of the earth's interior between the crust and the core, believed to consist of hot, dense silicate rocks.

phreatomagmatic eruption: also known as phreatic eruption—a volcanic eruption in which both magmatic gases and steam from groundwater are expelled in an explosion that resembles the shape of a rooster's tail.

pidgin: a grammatically simplified form of a language used for communication between people not sharing a common language.

plate tectonics: a theory explaining the structure of the earth's crust resulting from the interaction of rigid lithospheric plates that move slowly over the mantle.

Plinian: relating to or describing a type of explosive volcanic eruption in which a dark, narrow stream of gas and tephra is ejected from a vent to a height of several miles.

prahu: also spelled proa or prau, a type of sailing boat from Malaysia and Indonesia that may be sailed with either end at the front. It typically has a large triangular sail and an outrigger.

pyroclastic flow or surge: a ground-hugging avalance of hot ash, pumice, rock fragments, and volcanic gas that rushes down the side of a volcano as fast as 60 miles per hour or more. The temperature within a pyroclastic flow may be greater than 500 degrees Celsius.

seismic: of or relating to earthquakes or other vibrations of the earth and its crust.

stringer: a newspaper reporter not on the regular staff of a newspaper, usually hired on a part-time basis to report on events in a particular location.

subduction: the sideways and downward movement of the edge of a tectonic plate of the earth's crust into the mantle beneath another tectonic plate.

tectonic: of or relating to the structure of the earth's crust and the large-scale processes that take place within it.

tephra: the general term for fragments of volcanic rock and lava regardless of size that are blasted into the air by explosions or carried upward by hot gases in eruption columns or lava fountains.

trace: a line or pattern displayed by a measuring instrument using a moving pen to show the existence or nature of something that is being measured and recorded.

troupe: a group of entertainers who tour to different places.

tsunami: a long high sea wave caused by an earthquake, submarine landslide, or other disturbance.

SUGGESTED VOLCANO WEBSITES

Type the keyword *volcano* into your search engine, and the result is a list of 17 million sites, making it one of the more popular subjects on the Internet. The list includes sites from governments, university geology departments and other educational institutions, private organizations, fans of volcanology, movies and programs that feature volcanoes, even sites that show you how to make your own volcano. Here are a few useful sites:

VOLCANO WORLD
http://volcano.und.edu

This is the higher education, K–12, and public outreach project of the North Dakota Space Grant Consortium. It lists itself as the Internet's premier source of volcano information. The site features easily accessible sections including recent updates, current eruptions, FAQs, interviews, teaching and learning, glossary and terms, as well as links to additional sites.

U.S. GEOLOGICAL SURVEY VOLCANO HAZARDS PROGRAM
http://volcanoes.usgs.gov

The USGS is an unbiased, multi-disciplinary science organization of the federal government that focuses on biology, geography, geology, geospatial information, and water. It is dedicated to the timely, relevant, and impartial study of the landscape, natural resources, and natural hazards. The Volcano Hazards Program provides up-to-date information about volcano activity worldwide, emergency planning to reduce volcanic risk, and a variety of resources including photos, reports, FAQs, videos and other products, and educational information. The site is extensive and includes external links.

SMITHSONIAN INSTITUTION GLOBAL VOLCANISM NETWORK
www.volcano.si.edu/world

The Smithsonian Institution's site on volcanoes is extensive. It includes a wealth of information gathered and compiled by Smithsonian volcanologists over the past three decades.

MTU VOLCANOES PAGE
www.geo.mtu.edu/volcanoes

The Michigan Technological University Volcanoes Page is sponsored by the Keweenaw Volcano Observatory of Michigan Tech and is dedicated to providing scientific and educational information about volcanoes and their hazards as well as links to other sites.

WIKIPEDIA
en.wikipedia.org/wiki/Volcano

Wikipedia, the encyclopedia of the Internet, provides a good summary of how volcanoes are formed, the different types of volcanoes, and outside links to authoritative sites.

WOODS HOLE OCEANOGRAPHIC INSTITUTION
www.whoi.edu/page.do?pid=12461

Woods Hole Oceanographic Institution is the world's largest nonprofit oceanographic institution. This site includes a lot of useful information about volcanoes, with a focus on volcanoes formed in sea beds.

HOW VOLCANOES WORK
www.geology.sdsu.edu/how_volcanoes_work

This site developed by the Department of Geological Sciences, San Diego State University, is an educational resource that describes the science behind volcanoes and volcanic processes. It is sponsored by NASA under the auspices of Project ALERT (Augmented Learning Environment and Renewable Teaching) and is intended for the education of university students of geology and volcanolgy and teachers of earth science.

Bruce, Victoria. *No Apparent Danger: The True Story of Volcanic Disaster at Galeras and Nevado del Ruiz*. New York: HarperCollins, 2001.

Carson, Rob. *Mount St. Helens: the Eruption and Recovery of a Volcano*. Seattle: Sasquatch Books, 1990.

Decker, Robert, and Barbara Decker. *Volcanoes*. New York: W. H. Freeman, 2005.

Duffield, Wendell A. *Chasing Lava: A Geologist's Adventures at the Hawaiian Volcano Observatory*. Missoula, MT: Mountain Press Publishing Company, 2003.

Fisher, Richard V., and Grant Heiken and Jeffrey Hulen. *Volcanoes*. Princeton, NJ: Princeton University Press, 1998.

Francis, Peter, and Clive Oppenheimer. *Volcanoes*. New York: Oxford University Press, 2003.

Friedrich, Walter L. *Fire in the Sea. The Santorini Volcano: Natural History and the Legend of Atlantis*. Cambridge, England: Cambridge University Press, 2000.

Read, Donald. *The Power of News: The History of Reuters 1849–1989*. New York: Oxford University Press, 1992.

Rosi, Mauro, and Paolo Papale, Luca Lup, and Marco Stoppato. *Volcanoes*. Richmond Hill, Ontario: Firefly Books, 2003.

Scarth, Alwyn. *La Catastrophe: The Eruption of Mount Pelee, the Worst Volcanic Disaster of the 20th Century*. New York: Oxford University Press, 2004.

Schmincke, Hans-Ulrich. *Volcanism*. Frankfurt, Germany: Springer, 2005.

Severin, Timothy. *The Spice Islands Voyage: The Quest for Alfred Wallace, the Man Who Shared Darwin's Discovery of Evolution*. New York: Carroll & Graf, 1997.

Shermer, Michael. *In Darwin's Shadow: The Life and Science of Alfred Russel Wallace*. New York: Oxford University Press, 2002.

Sigurdsson, Haraldur, and Bruce Houghton, Hazel Rymer, John x, and Steve McNutt. *Encyclopedia of Volcanoes*. San Diego:

Thompson, Dick. *Volcano Cowboys. The Rocky Evolution of a Dangerous Science*. New York: St. Martin's Griffin, 2002.

Winchester, Simon. *Krakatoa: The Day the World Exploded August 27, 1883*. New York: HarperCollins, 2003.

Zeilinga de Boer, Jelle, and Donald Theodore Sanders and Robert D. Ballard. *Volcanoes in Human History: The Far-Reaching Effects of Major Eruptions*. Princeton, NJ: Princeton University Press, 2004.